Soul Friendship

Soul Friendship

A Practical Theology of Spiritual Direction

Nigel Rooms and Adrian Chatfield

CANTERBURY PRESS
Norwich

© Nigel Rooms and Adrian Chatfield 2019

First published in 2019 by the Canterbury Press Norwich
Editorial office
3rd Floor, Invicta House
108–114 Golden Lane
London EC1Y 0TG, UK
www.canterburypress.co.uk

Canterbury Press is an imprint of Hymns Ancient & Modern Ltd
(a registered charity)

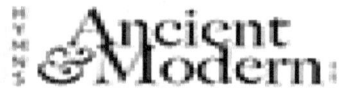

Hymns Ancient & Modern® is a registered trademark of
Hymns Ancient & Modern Ltd
13A Hellesdon Park Road, Norwich,
Norfolk NR6 5DR, UK

All rights reserved. No part of this publication may be reproduced,
stored in a retrieval system, or transmitted,in any form
or by any means, electronic, mechanical,
photocopying or otherwise, without the prior permission of
the publisher, Canterbury Press.

The Authors have asserted their right under the Copyright, Designs and
Patents Act 1988 to be identified as the Authors of this Work

Unless otherwise stated in the text, scripture quotations are from the New
Revised Standard Version of the Bible, Anglicized Edition, copyright ©
1989, 1995 by the Division of Christian Education of the National
Council of the Churches of Christ in the USA. Used by permission.

All rights reserved.

British Library Cataloguing in Publication data

A catalogue record for this book is available
from the British Library

978 1-78622-156-8

Nigel:
To Graham Pigott, who planted the seed that germinated into this book. I acknowledge here my debt to his Christian joy, inspiration and challenge.

Adrian:
To my wife Jill, whose patience has known no bounds when I have been under writing pressure over the years. She is my sharpest critic and best friend in the enterprise of life.

Contents

About the Authors ix
Introduction 1

1 God and Spiritual Direction 19
2 The Human Person in Companionship 42
3 Jesus, God Incarnate; 'Turning Up' 61
4 Salvation and Transformation: Towards Union 77
5 The Holy Spirit and Companionship 99
6 Theological Approaches to the Bible in
   Accompaniment 119
7 Spiritual Direction and the Traditions of Christianity 137
8 The Church and Spiritual Direction 157
9 Towards a Practical Theology of Spiritual Direction 177

Bibliography 188
Index of Names and Subjects 195

About the Authors

Nigel Rooms has been ordained for almost 30 years, is presently based in Leicester and is an honorary Canon of Christchurch Cathedral, Arusha, Tanzania. He holds masters and doctoral degrees in theology and mission. He worked in senior training and development positions in the Diocese of Southwell and Nottingham and, with the Church Mission Society, now helps local churches to shape their long-term future. He is editor of the journal *Practical Theology*. He has been a spiritual director for ten years and is a Priest Associate of the Sisters of the Love of God at Fairacres, Oxford. Nigel is married to Karen, who is also an Anglican priest, and they are mightily blessed with two adult sons, Joe and Alistair. Nigel's allotment is a source of joy throughout the year.

Adrian Chatfield is a Trinidadian priest who was sent as 'a missionary to the English' in 1983. He has been a parish priest and theological educator in the UK and South Africa, and was involved in setting up and running the Simeon Centre for Prayer and the Spiritual Life at Ridley Hall, Cambridge. His doctoral work was on spirituality in Caribbean literature, and he has been a spiritual director and trainer since the early 1990s. He was a member of the National Fresh Expressions team, and continues to encourage new forms of church and pioneer ministers. His spiritual 'cave' is long-distance running, where he has discovered a new joy in prayer. Adrian is married to Jill, who is also an

Anglican priest, and they have a son and daughter and four grandchildren. Adrian loves searching for and photographing wildflowers, fungi and birds.

Introduction

Spiritual direction is a burgeoning and multi-faceted ministry across the churches in the UK and the wider western world, including many Protestant denominations. The publishing of books related to spiritual direction has continued unabated over the past 20-30 years, so why have we written another book on the subject?

Like all authors perhaps, we think our book is a little bit different. We know that there is a lot of writing on the 'how to' of spiritual direction, but there is less on the theological grounding of the practice. That is why we think it would be helpful in current thinking about spiritual direction to look at the question of what is theological about two people meeting regularly to discern the movement of God in the life of one of them. We hope by the end of the book that everyone involved in being directed and directing (as beginner or experienced) will find a valuable theological resource that can strengthen the depth and breadth of our practice. Ultimately this should increase our commitment to spiritual direction, develop our capacity for receiving and offering direction and enhance the quality of what happens in the direction session and beyond. We offer this work also as a theological *apologia* for spiritual direction and expect that it will reinforce the teaching and reflection on it in many places.

In this Introduction we will discuss definitions of spiritual direction and the limits of what we are attempting. We know that we don't write in a vacuum, so we'll spend some time thinking about sources for this work, both primary and secondary. We will take a 'practical theology' approach to the subject, so we'll need to spell out the methodology, as sometimes there is considerable confusion about it. We'll set out some current changes in the context of the Christian Church in the western world as a background for understanding the vital importance of spiritual direction and then we'll introduce the rest of the book.

First, though, a word to position the authors. We are both white male Anglican priests firmly in the second half of life. Having said that, we have considerable experience of living and working cross-culturally in the Caribbean and Africa and are, hopefully, conscious of the biases we may bring to this project. We have both been directed as praying disciples of Jesus for many years and offer direction to others. Theologically we both wish to take reflection on experience utterly seriously, hence our approach in this book, which we'll say more about later. Our method of writing has been to share out the initial creation of each chapter and then to agree (sometimes after serious further thought and discussion) the final text together.[1] So we'll use both singular and plural first-person pronouns at different points as we proceed.

Definitions, metaphors and nomenclature

Inevitably there are as many definitions of spiritual direction as authors writing about it. Often definitions expand into explaining the purpose or aim of direction, which is not unreasonable but which is probably also the reason for the variety of definitions. There is clearly not one outcome for what happens through spiritual direction. When writing a leaflet introducing spiritual companionship some years ago,

---

[1] Nigel was the first writer of the Introduction and Chapters 2, 3, 6 and 8, while Adrian initiated Chapters 1, 4, 5, 7 and 9.

our group came up very quickly with more than ten concrete transformations it offers, drawn from our experience. (A full reproduction and explication of this text is in Chapter 8.) However, several authors such as William Barry, William Connolly and Kenneth Leech are agreed that on reading the Christian tradition they have come to understand its ultimate purpose or aim as the *union* of the praying subject of direction with God.

Formally and factually, spiritual direction is two people meeting regularly to focus on the spiritual life of one of them, with certain agreed boundaries of time, place and subject matter. 'Spiritual life' here is defined as 'the life of the whole person directed towards God' (Leech, 1994, p. 30). Informally, spiritual direction can occur fairly spontaneously in many settings – after church over coffee, on a car journey, at a pastoral visit. Our focus in this book is on the former without ignoring totally the possibilities of the latter.

Let's begin with the Jesuits, and Barry and Connolly's definition:

> help given by one Christian to another which enables that person to pay attention to God's personal communication to him or her, to respond to this personally communicating God, to grow in intimacy with this God, and to live out the consequences of the relationship. (1986, p. 8)

While being slightly wooden and individualized, Barry and Connolly are not over- or under-claiming what occurs in direction and are relating it to the *revelation* of God. Personally I prefer the word 'movement' to 'communication' since the latter might imply, at least to some readers, the use of words alone (which we won't preclude, just not apply all the time). Movement is no less real, but harder to pin down, and is related to my understanding of God as a verb rather than a noun: God as the flow in which we participate. We will say more about this in Chapter 1.

Martin Thornton is much more succinct: 'Spiritual direction is the application of theology to the life of prayer' (1984, p.1). Prayer, as he points out, is a 'this-world' activity that extends into all areas of life. Here we have the beginnings of permission for our approach to the subject of this book since it points us to understanding what happens in the direction room: 'God-talk' or the naming of the movement of God in the life of the directee in the world. This is the act of doing theology not as an academic theoretical exercise but as an urgent practical matter. As Evagrius Ponticus (345–99 CE) is famously quoted as saying, a theologian is 'one whose prayer is true'. Thus we could claim that spiritual direction is ultimately a form of practical theology.

Leech importantly places spiritual direction in the prophetic tradition, which does not reduce the practice purely to the realm of the personal: 'Spiritual direction is concerned with healing and reconciliation ... with the transformation of consciousness' (1994, p.182). Spiritual direction, since the Holy Spirit is involved, encompasses questions of power and therefore politics, and is connected to the holistic nature of what happens when the Kingdom of God comes near or is 'at hand' (that is, never graspable by being *in* the hand).

So perhaps summing up we might say that spiritual direction is two people attending to and naming the movement of God in the spiritual life of one of them, for the ultimate good of that individual and the world they inhabit.

So much for definitions; perhaps even more useful are metaphors for spiritual direction, since a picture is worth a thousand words. Indeed even the names we give the practice are metaphorical, so we'll need to address the nomenclature question here as well.

Thornton begins with a biblical metaphor – that of the 'training of the spiritual athlete' (1984, p. 16) taken from 1

INTRODUCTION

Corinthians 9.24-27 and Acts 24.16. This is where we gain the word 'ascetical' – to exercise or train. Perhaps Thornton's most powerful metaphor is a paradoxical and forensic one: 'Love on the cold stone slab' (p. 31). The emphasis here is on classification and diagnosis all within a relationship of love for the directee. Perhaps these are particularly male metaphors and the question of gender in direction is one we will return to in Chapter 2.

For now, it is also worth sharing Margaret Guenther's metaphors. Her book *Holy Listening* really only contains metaphors and she has one for the relationship itself and two for the role of director. She understands spiritual direction as hospitality – sharing space, place, silence and stories among other things. She thinks of the director as 'teacher' (a traditional picture – but a 'Socratic' teacher who asks questions rather than gives answers) and also more suggestively as 'midwife' who brings something new to birth in the directee.

My own preference is for a fire metaphor. I have always loved bonfires, and I know they need to be hot enough to live and require fairly constant attention to continue burning well. The fire of God burns within and without us. So I imagine a campfire scene where we are attending to three fires, not just one, and yet one person is making sure the campfires continue to burn. Somehow as we attend to the fire of God burning in the room outside us this also kindles the fires burning within our own hearts (cf. Luke 24.32).

The cover picture we chose for our book resonates, we hope, with this metaphor. We liked it because of the way the light, perhaps from a fire, plays both in the centre and on the figures. It also creates some shadows that are necessary, and there is an ambiguity about just how many people are together. In our experience, spiritual accompaniment is about much more than just two people in a room together.

So to nomenclature. Direction as a word is often objected to by some practitioners because of the baggage it carries – the perception is of 'command and control', of demanding certain actions and responses on the part of the directee. Personally I think it is redeemable from this state for several reasons – first we abandon the traditional word for this task at our peril since it was hard won over many centuries; second in the creative arts (e.g. film, theatre) a director is essential to the overall truth, beauty and goodness of the event being directed. Finally, it is about moving in a certain direction and not others – even if the path is not that certain or clear there are boundary markers and the need is to keep moving towards the goal of union. And there is the sense that the director has some knowledge of the road ahead and how to navigate the distractions, obstacles and by-ways.

Other popular names for the same practice are accompaniment and the related word companionship, guidance and soul friendship, even soul physician. Accompaniment is often related to the story of Jesus walking alongside the two disciples on the Emmaus Road in Luke 24. Not least because the story ends when they break bread together, which is the root of the word 'companion' – to share bread in Latin and French. A guide is not that far from director, at least as we have understood that term. Someone who knows the terrain and can explain how it is to be navigated, what the pitfalls might be and what is coming over the horizon. Soul friend, as Leech points out, is a translation of the Irish Gaelic word *anmchara* (1994, p. 46) and has passed into popular usage now as 'anamchara'. While something may be lost in translation here, given that friendship in popular terms is not entirely what is happening in the direction relationship, nevertheless the placing of soul with friend opens up a creative world of possibilities while also placing limits on that friendship. With physician we are back to diagnosis and treatment – on Thornton's 'cold stone slab'.

We wish to allow the usage of all possible nomenclature or terminology in this book since to limit ourselves to one overall

INTRODUCTION

metaphor is to reduce the possibilities of what a spiritual direction relationship is for. While mainly using spiritual direction, director and directee, we will also speak of soul friendship, companionship, companion and even pilgrim for those coming to direction.

A final word about our focus in this book. Companions and pilgrims coming together in spiritual direction are both praying people, and some of what they speak of is their experience of prayer. The task we have set ourselves here is to reflect theologically on the relationship of these two within the flow of God and not specifically on prayer itself. This is not to say we won't need to draw on theological resources about prayer, just that this will not be the centre of this work.

Sources for this book

Following Isaac Newton and others before him we recognize first of all that everything we do in this work is because we are 'standing on the shoulders of giants'.

Those giants are traceable right back to the origins of Christianity, particularly the Desert Fathers and Mothers of the fourth century and those in the monastic movement that followed them. These are what we call 'primary' sources – like Evagrius Ponticus.

One of the joys of the practice of spiritual companionship is that it seems to cross denominational boundaries more easily than some other tasks of our different churches. Perhaps because we are all so thirsty. We hope that we have written this book in ecumenical perspective, drawing on Catholic, Protestant and some Orthodox sources. Speaking as a priest of a denomination that is both reformed and catholic it has been pressed home to me recently, given the dire predictions about future membership of so-called 'mainstream' denominations in the West, that their long-term sustainability is predicated on sources from the length and breadth of the traditions of the whole Church. An example is the amazing reach of the principles of Ignatian spirituality over the past 40 years. A few years ago I was with a group of highly significant Protestant denominational leaders in the USA who had all made deep and helpful changes in their respective church bodies – and to a person they all spoke of discerning what God is doing via the Ignatian language of consolation and desolation.

As well as the giants of the primary sources, there are other giants who have written more recently whom we need to acknowledge here, not least because they have done a lot of the groundwork on the primary sources for us. Kenneth Leech is one such giant whom we have already quoted. Chapter 2 of his now classic book *Soul Friend* is entitled 'Spiritual Direction in the Christian Tradition' (1994, pp. 30-85). It is a magisterial review of approaches to the subject across the denominations and centuries and stands the test of time. It is worth noting briefly here his synthesis on the nature of spiritual director as we will return to these ideas from time to time in the book and especially in Chapter 7. There are five characteristics – soul friends are possessed by the Spirit, experienced, learned, discerning and always 'giving way to the Holy Spirit'.

While Martin Thornton in *Spiritual Direction: A Practical Introduction* might overstate the amount of knowledge needed to be an effective director I believe he is another more recent 'giant'. Most useful is his diagrammatic representation of the sources and historical schools of spiritual direction (1984, pp. 136-7).

Other secondary sources that have engaged with the theology of spiritual companionship are mainly from the USA and are both further Protestant and Catholic partners for our task in this book. Since Jesuit approaches to direction have taken root so deeply we need to take account of both William Barry SJ, *Spiritual Direction and the Encounter with God: A Theological*

Inquiry, and William Reiser SJ, *Seeking God in All Things: Theology and Spiritual Direction*. These books, while making useful points, have a somewhat limited scope in relation to our practical theology approach and are answering some questions from the mid-twentieth century which perhaps are not so pressing now. A helpful introduction to a more Reformed style of companionship is Angela Reed, Richard Osmer and Marcus Smucker, *Spiritual Companioning: A Guide to Protestant Theology and Practice*. We will spend some time interacting with some of these secondary sources through the book and especially in Chapter 8.

Practical theology and spiritual direction

As we begin this book it will be important for some readers to ask what kind of task spiritual direction is and what is the best method of studying, reflecting and learning it. Other readers less concerned with our theological method in writing this book could easily skip this section. We have already seen that companionship is *processual*: it begins somewhere and has an overall goal (even if that goal of union will look different for each person who attains it and isn't gained in a straight line from here to there); and that it has to do with God. We might go further and say that it is ultimately about knowledge of God – where that knowledge is fully rounded and holistic in the biblical sense of knowing and being known, even possessing and being possessed. It is therefore also about knowledge gained through experience, or as Barry prefers it, *encounter* (2004, p. 23).

Thus we need a way of thinking about knowledge and how it is gained. I have written elsewhere on this subject (Rooms, 2011, pp. 82–3) and will recycle that work here in more accessible language, without repeating it word for word, along with developing it slightly in a significant way for our purposes here.

We have to begin with the Greek philosopher Aristotle

(384–322 BCE) who divided the subject of knowledge into three different ways of knowing – he called them *theoria, praxis* and *poiesis*. It is important to understand each of these three ideas in Aristotle's thinking in turn.

Theoria happens in one's mind alone – it is objective thought apart from the human body. It proceeds via *episteme*, which is about spending time within any subject and reflecting on what is good, true and beautiful such that wisdom (*sophia*) about that subject is the result. We might think of *pure* mathematics as an example. Aristotle elevated this kind of knowing above all others as he felt it was an end in itself and needed no further justification, or indeed any action resulting from it. His views on this have been highly influential in how knowledge is understood and gained in western thought right up to today. It is worth noting that *theoria* is close to our English word theory but it isn't quite the same thing; more of that in a moment.

Praxis is quite different since it is about how life in society at large is conducted and it aims at human flourishing (and is therefore always incomplete). It necessarily has to do with morality, ethics and politics. It begins with some problem or issue and utilizes *phronesis*, which does translate fairly accurately into English as 'practical wisdom' – not quite the same thing as common sense but not far off. We can already see a connection with our subject here since judgement and discernment are required when the goal is human flourishing. What we can be sure of is that *praxis* is definitely *not* the same thing as practice or taking action. We can't underline this difference enough and will return to it soon.

Poiesis is principally concerned with the making of things and is therefore what we call craft, in the traditional sense of the knowledge acquired in a long apprenticeship in order to master the craft of, say, cabinet making. The reader will notice that the word is very close to our word poetry and indeed it relates to the creativity involved in making any artefact – a painting, poem, song, play, piece of music, the list is endless. *Poiesis* is arrived at by employing *techne* or skill (and of course is where we derive the words technique and technology from).

So much for the origins of these ways of knowing in Greek philosophy. Unfortunately Aristotle's elevation of *theoria* above the others was magnified over the centuries, more especially in the West. Here is not the place to go into how this happened, suffice to say that we ended up thinking that how others came to know more (in other words, learning) was about passing on theoretical knowledge (which was disembodied and not related to actual physical experience). The theory which was generated was then put to work in practice or action. When combined with an emphasis on the importance of the rational, thinking individual in the period of the Enlightenment (c. 1650-1950) we were left with a toxic mix of half-truths about what it is to know anything and to learn new things. We still have a legacy of such ideas in the overall way we organize, for instance, training for ordination. To put it somewhat crudely, students are 'front-loaded' with everything they might need to know before they are sent out to 'put it into practice' during their ministerial life.

Several things now need to be said. First, we are not rejecting *theoria* altogether. Leech and Thornton have separately shown that some theoretical knowledge of God and God's ways is necessary in spiritual direction. This knowledge, however, given what we don't and will never know about God, is always limited and partial. It has so often to be left at the door of the 'mystery' of God or, as the unknown medieval English writer put it, *The Cloud of Unknowing*. What we are rejecting here is a linear trajectory from not knowing to being filled up with knowledge that can then be practised. Yes, we need a limited, partial and theoretical 'minimum knowledge base' to draw from, but much more important is the space between theory and action which is filled up with *praxis* and *poiesis*.

Let's think some more about these two ways of knowing.

Today, given the work of several key scholars on the subject, *praxis* has become the work done to generate knowledge between what we might call action and reflection (where reflection is standing back from the action, noticing what happened and trying to make sense of it). This knowledge is what we name practical wisdom. These two, action and reflection, are in an eternal virtuous circle without beginning or end and we can join that circle at any point. We can say, 'no one learns from experience; we only learn from experience that is reflected upon and articulated to another.'

Theology, then, whether we call it practical or systematic (and there is a much larger and longer debate about the relationship of these terms), has to take physical embodied experience seriously. This is particularly the case when learning about prayer and our spiritual life with another person. Spiritual direction occurs in this betwixt and between place, in the space created by action and reflection (scholars call this a 'liminal' space – literally an 'edge' between two states of being), and it needs all the help it can get in that space especially on the side of the reflection.

Practical theology therefore is always an inter-disciplinary arena of study drawing on support from, for instance, sociology, psychology, social anthropology and many others fields of inquiry. In this book, while we will distinguish spiritual guidance from various forms of counselling and psychotherapy, that does not mean we exclude their contribution altogether from developing our practical wisdom on how best to proceed. On the other hand, reflection on what happens in spiritual direction will also include the Christian disciplines of biblical and doctrinal theology. Overall practical theology asks the question: 'How then shall we live?' In relation to our task the question is: 'How then shall we companion?' We have to understand this as a fundamentally theological question.

Increasingly as I have come to work with these ideas I have realized that *praxis* and *poiesis* are much more intimately related and should really be held together. Apprenticeship in a craft such as, say, tailoring or carpentry always takes place in a *community*. It is about the acquisition of good and effective habits that are agreed upon by that community. All human communities are full of politics and power games by their very definition and every apprentice will both learn the accepted habits of the community and, if a good apprentice, will innovate and change those habits for the better. And the community if it is a wise one (with effective political process) will accept those changes and innovations for the sake of its future. Thus *phronesis* and *techne* go intimately together in the 'community of practice' which agrees how we shall direct the spiritual lives of others.

Poiesis therefore is vital to spiritual direction. Creativity and even playfulness in, for example, art, music and poetry can aid the journey towards union with God. We are talking about spiritual direction as a *craft* here and it is worth thinking about how, say, a piece of art is physically created by the artist or how a beautiful wooden cabinet comes into being. While the creator has a general end in mind, the work proceeds by moving into the fine detail (a brush stroke, a mortise and tenon joint) and then out again to see the whole. From this 'in/out' movement the whole emerges which may or may not end up looking like the original design, given the vagaries of the paint or the wood being used, for instance. So with prayer and spiritual direction, which proceed in the same way by moving in close and out to reflect before making another intervention.

Practical theology, therefore, as an approach to our subject liberates us. In that further sense it is the appropriate methodology for our work since liberation is also one of the fruits of prayer and good spiritual guidance. Through practical theology we are freed to be in a fluid rather than solid world, where nothing happens by chance and all experience can be drawn into the fullness of God's activity. And it is to God that we now turn.

God and the contemporary context for spiritual direction

It is much more than 20 years since Kenneth Leech published the revised edition of *Soul Friend*; the original version was published in 1977. Some things, like the long Christian tradition on direction, have not changed that much since he was writing. Other things have changed massively.

What is much clearer now than when Leech and Thornton were writing is what we can call the end, or in some places, the 'twilight' of Christendom. This ending is allied to the transformation of the period called the Enlightenment (or in some circles, 'modernity') into something else which in our day hasn't quite emerged yet. Christendom is a settlement between the political State and the Christian Church which has taken many forms, but which essentially means the State through its power guarantees a plausibility and safety structure for the existence of the Church. Thus, to use an idea of George Lings, in Christendom the prevailing culture rolls people into church which exists at the bottom of a cultural valley, as it were. When this situation ceases to exist, the Church finds itself at the top of a cultural hill where people are rolled away from it. The Church simply cannot wait for people to turn up, however attractive their liturgical worship is. I and many others see this new situation as offering new challenges and opportunities for the Church, since God, radically, does not change. Others act as if they deny the reality of what is happening or make knee-jerk responses borne from anxiety about what we are losing.

Theological reflection has a response to this situation from a realization and even movement that began among theologians in the middle of the twentieth century. These scholars recovered the sense that God is active always and everywhere, within, but more especially beyond the Church itself. It is easy to see how this understanding was lost in the era of Christendom where the world and the Church were much more closely one and the same thing.

God, so this thinking goes, is missionary by God's *very nature*, an idea which in Latin is the *Missio Dei*. God creates and sustains the universe in every moment out of a superfluity of abundance in God (we are ultimately theists, not deists). God crosses the boundary of Godself to make this other, the world which is not God, and the people of that world God constantly loves into being. God never gives up on this other, even when people reject and rebel against their creator. So God continues to cross the boundary and God's son descends to become one of the people and take humanity into Godself (Phil. 2.5-11). Creation and salvation are intimately connected as movements outward from God to the other and back again.

This brings us to a fairly well-known key principle for the Church after Christendom, which is that it is not the Church of God that has a mission in the world, but the God of mission that has Church in the world. The task of the Church is therefore to find out what God is doing and join in.[2]

This is what scholars have called a 'paradigm shift' – a whole new way of looking at the world – as when we realized from Galileo that the sun, not the earth, was at the centre of our solar system, or when we first saw a picture of the earth from space. Everything has to change around this new knowledge.

For the Church this paradigm shift turns her inside out. The task is to discover what God is up to in the community and the world – both locally and globally. This is a task of *discernment*. Which of course is at the heart of the spiritual direction relationship.

So if spiritual direction was an urgent task for Leech and Thornton in their day, we believe it is an even more urgent task

---

[2] I have seen these statements attributed to several different authors in various books and repeat them here without referencing them as they are generally agreed across the literature.

today. In Chapter 8 we shall see spiritual companionship as a *fractal* of the task of the whole Church and, we believe, at the very centre of responding to the changes that are upon us. A fern leaf demonstrates the fractal principle. Every tiny piece of the fern is shaped in the same way as the next piece of the leaf and the whole frond itself. If we can learn how to place effective spiritual direction at the heart of what it is to be the Church, we have a chance of the Church thriving in some form in the West in the next 30–50 years.

The contents and arrangement of this book

Having set out our stall as one of developing an understanding of the crucial nature of spiritual direction through *phronesis* arising from *praxis* and *poiesis*, we now introduce the rest of the book. As craftspeople we are always learning and so it is worth pointing out that each chapter ends with a set of reflection questions which can be used individually or in group discussion in course work on spiritual direction, for example.

We will begin at the source and end of all things in God. There are many pressing questions with regard to God which spiritual companionship both addresses and raises which will need to be explored. The Trinitarian nature of the Christian God has a profound effect on the moment-by-moment movement in the companionship meeting as well as how we relate to God's presence and absence with us and in us and the world.

After God comes humanity – or to use the technical term, anthropology. Who are the human beings sitting together in a room discerning the movement of God among them? How much or little might we expect of them, both as individuals, as Christian community and as part of the human race? If they are at one and the same time bearers of the image of God and open to all sorts of sinful and addictive behaviours, what implications does this paradox have for them and their longing for freedom in union with God? What about the place of gender and the body in direction? Psychology and inter-personal dynamics also have a role to play.

Related to these questions are those of salvation or 'soteriology'. We start thinking about these issues by looking at who Christ is and is not, as the answers will be powerful drivers of how we understand the paradoxes inherent in spiritual direction. The incarnation and the whole movement of the paschal mystery have important consequences for embodiment in the Christian life and how we might expect to plumb some depths in prayer and companionship.

We have said that the purpose of spiritual guidance is union with God for the pilgrim. But what does this mean? What is it that Christ has achieved for us on the cross? What are the implications of union for the process of ongoing sanctification and what some theologians call *theosis*, the divinization of humanity in God? Where do repentance, reconciliation and forgiveness fit with soul friendship?

The place of the Holy Spirit in direction is given a further chapter and questions of power, 'politics' and the potential for abuse in companioning must be raised here.

The Bible and the Christian tradition are dealt with in the next two chapters as important sources for spiritual companionship. The Bible can be used well and abused in direction, as can the tradition.

Finally we address spiritual guidance and the Church – or ecclesiology as it is known. Where does spiritual direction best lie within the Church? Is it for everyone all the time? How do we address acutely practical questions like accountability and professionalization?

In conclusion we will sum up the overall argument and share what we feel are the unifying factors in a practical theology of spiritual direction. No doubt we will be left with more questions and so we'll indicate what further theological work might need to be done.

Reflection and questions

- Reading through the various definitions and metaphors for spiritual direction, which do you prefer? Why not try to write your own definition and/or work on your preferred metaphor?

- How do you respond to the stated importance of *praxis*, *phronesis* and *poiesis?* Do you notice the in/out movement in your own crafting of prayer and spiritual direction? How might the ideas of spiritual direction as craft and progressing in prayer as apprenticeship be helpful?

- What are the further implications of turning the Church inside out to join in with what God is already doing? Do you agree that spiritual direction can be a fractal, a microcosm of what needs to happen in the whole Church? How might understanding its place in the Church from this perspective strengthen our resolve to develop it and increase the resource given to it?

- What are you looking for from this book? Are there particular questions you'd like answers to? Most of the chapters stand alone, so where would you like to begin?

1

God and Spiritual Direction

In this chapter we will reflect on how we relate to a hospitable, dynamic God who is here and who draws near, longing to be known. In seeking to know God, we search for the languages that will help us respond, while recognizing that our relationship with God may also be characterized by distance, pain or silence.

A God who comes near

Our life as Christian disciples is often likened to a journey or pilgrimage shared with companions whose relationship grows and matures as we travel together. Our little band of pilgrims is, of course, the Church of God. By beginning with this metaphor, we state a key theological truth, a 'given'. At the same time, we raise a theological conundrum, and both of these take us straight to the heart of a theology of spiritual direction.

The given is the fact that we journey with God, and towards God, though God is more than merely a companion. The conundrum is that the God with whom we journey is the God whom we sometimes know but often lose sight of. This is a God whom we search and yearn for on a good day, but then flee, ignore or rail against. This God is the only reason why we journey but equally the one about whom we are at times also most doubtful. It is the conundrum of faith.

The poet Walter de la Mare (1873-1956) captures this conundrum wonderfully in the best known of his poems for children, 'Someone', which begins with a knock and continues with a profound sense of presence:

> Someone came knocking
> At my wee, small door;
> Someone came knocking;
> I'm sure-sure-sure ...

Yet the poem ends with an absence, a silence:

> So I know not who came knocking,
> At all, at all, at all.[3]

Like de la Mare, those who seek spiritual direction wrestle with a God who cannot easily or always be found, a God with whom they may have had profound encounters, yet who seems often to be just beyond reach, or even to have engineered that absence. A God who hides. The one thing that characterizes all such spiritual exploration is a sense of the 'is-ness' of God, of God's presence *for them*, of encounters with that God, and the elusiveness and unpredictability of God. Yearning and searching for a vision of God marks most spiritual journeys, and the heart of spiritual direction is the accompaniment of those who search. As spiritual companions, we stand equally alongside those who long to encounter God, those who lament a sense of the absence of God, and those who delight in or wrestle with the presence of a God who is both with and beyond them. The greatest joy and challenge of direction is the uniqueness of each person's experience of God, and to work with what each person brings to us.

Kenneth Kirk (1886–1954), Bishop of Oxford and spiritual theologian, began a series of lectures on the Vision of God by quoting the words of Irenaeus of Lyons: *'Gloria enim Dei vivens*

---

[3] Poem accessed from 'Someone – Poem by Walter de la Mare', *PoemHunter.com*, www.poemhunter.com/poem/some-one/ (accessed 23.4.2019). Grateful acknowledgement is made to the Literary Trustees of Walter de la Mare and the Society of Authors as their representative.

homo; vita autem hominis visio Dei' (1931, p. 1) – the glory of God is a living person, and (at the heart of) the life of that person is the vision of God. When I first began to struggle with the Scriptures in the Sesotho language as a mission partner in Southern Africa, I had to read in public the story of Moses' encounter with the 'God who is' at the burning bush in the desert. In this African tongue, God is no philosopher speaking about pure being, essence against mere existence. Here God says *'Ke nna Ya-Leng-Teng'* (Bibele e Halalelang, Ex. 3.14), I am the one who is really here, implicitly, here with you and for you, willing and available.

Even more significantly perhaps, this present and available God is a God who approaches, who takes the first step. This is why the doctrine of the inspiration of the Holy Scriptures lies primarily not in the fact that they are accurate in some scientific or historical sense, nor in the nature of their transmission. It lies in our understanding that through them, God chooses to make Godself known, a theme that will be more fully developed in Chapter 6. God is a self-revealing God, and when Christians pray, 'Their experience of participation in a divine dialogue is an experience of a God who actively and always wills to be among us, God Emmanuel' (Doctrine Commission, p. 109). John V. Taylor is making exactly the same point, albeit of the body corporate, when he describes the Holy Spirit as the 'chief actor in the historic mission of the Christian church' (2004, p. 280).

In classical systematic theologies, God is sovereign and makes the first move. This view places God outside or beyond the created order. The distinction between creator and created, redeemer and redeemed, empowerer and empowered is key to Christian theology, but in the task of accompaniment it creates a predicament, a distance, a gulf that cannot be crossed. At worst God becomes entirely unreachable, and at best terrifyingly remote. In protecting the integrity of God, we run the risk of alienating those who long for the divine embrace.

A theology of spiritual direction does not negate the sovereignty of God, but binds it together with the doctrine of grace. Because of this, we confidently teach that God can be known because God wills to be known. God can be sought because we are constantly sought by God. God is both knowable and approachable.

God comes near as Three-in-One

Many of the debates which have bedevilled the Church down the ages have been generated by an imperfect vision which has sought to contain our knowledge of God at one end of a polarity:[4] revelation, or reason? Scripture, or tradition? Word, or Sacrament? The shared insights of the whole Church of God throughout history show by contrast that God can be accessed in a diversity of ways consonant with the diversity embodied in the creation. Those diversities in turn tell us something key about the character of God: God can only be known when known as One-in-Three.

The Church's proclamation of God as Holy and Blessed Trinity, which took the early Church so long to formulate, is the *framework* for all our encounters. It is the whole against which we measure our partial engagement, the act of worship which enlarges our celebration, the doctrine against which we lay all our partial theological insights. To know God as One-in-Three and Three-in-One is to know with the saints down the ages:

- that all of God is involved in the creative, redemptive and transformative movement that is the cosmos;
- that this movement is a reflection of the interpersonal unity and interaction within the Three in One;

---

4 A polarity is like a battery – two outwardly opposing ideas which are irreconcilable but when deliberately held together in tension produce energy for transformation.

- God is a verb, not a noun – a personal embrace or flow, dynamic, never static (Bevans and Schroeder, 2011, p. 9);
- that unity is fully expressed and experienced in relationship: community is at the heart of what it truly means to be One; and
- that the unity of the Godhead is not exclusive, but inclusive and hospitable.

That is why Trinitarian formulae can never be mechanical or pseudo-scientific. They invite us to join in with the flow of God. We are invited to join in with the life of God rather than simply to learn about God. Spiritual theology demands engaged response, not abstract understanding. As the Orthodox bishop-theologian John Zizioulas says: 'Trinitarian theology has profound existential consequences' (2010, p. 485).

So as we explore in more depth what it means to meet this God who comes near, we will look at three facets of that approach:

- The divine dance, in which we celebrate the presence of God with us and for us.
- The beauty of God, in which we wonder at the glory and majesty of God.
- Word and sacramental acts and actions, which mediate the presence of God, thus revealing God to us.

The divine dance: celebration

The twentieth century saw a proliferation of dance language around the nature of God, the character of Christian worship, and our sharing in the mission of God towards the world. Sydney Carter's 'Lord of the Dance' (1963), Graham Maule and John Bell's 'Dance and Sing' (1987) and Graham Kendrick's 'Teach me to dance' (1993) are notable examples. This was not new language. The medieval carol 'Tomorrow shall be my dancing day' speaks of Jesus calling his true love to the dance and ends with:

> Then up to heaven I did ascend,
> Where now I dwell in sure substance
> On the right hand of God, that man
> May come unto the general dance.

Among theologians and spiritual writers, Jürgen Moltmann, Eugene Peterson (2005, p. 44ff), Steve Bevans and Roger Schroeder (2011, p. 17) and Tim Keller stand out. Keller, overturning a long-held conservative tendency to avoid non-biblical language in theology, comments that

> each of the divine persons centres upon the others. None demands that the others revolve around him. Each voluntarily circles the other two, pouring love, delight, and adoration into them. Each person of the Trinity loves, adores, defers to, and rejoices in the others. That creates a dynamic, pulsating dance of joy and love. (2008, p. 214)

Such language refers back to the Greek term *perichoresis* (literally meaning 'to go around'), used in verb form by Bishop Gregory of Nazianzus (c. 329-90) to explain the interrelationship[5] of the two natures of Christ, then by John of Damascus (c. 675-749) to refer to the interrelationship of the persons of the Trinity. The defensive function of the term is to protect the doctrine against accusations of tritheism, the classic Islamic charge that Christians have three gods. Its more positive function is to draw

---

5 The old texts call this 'interpenetration' but this is a rarely used word in modern English. 'Interrelationship' doesn't mean quite the same because it does not depict the movement in community (the dance) between Father, Son and Holy Spirit, but it has greater clarity for us.

us into the dynamic presence of God:

- First, the heart of God, Father, Son and Spirit are in continuous loving communication. That which one wills, the others will. What one does, the others share in. The three persons of the Trinity are united in their distinctiveness, and complement each other.
- It is the nature of love to give unstintingly. Because the divine love is creative, the will to create has always existed – 'before the foundation of the world'. The abundant love of God is creative not out of necessity but out of nature.
- Love intends a relationship with all that it creates. When that love is fractured or broken, love persists until the relationship is restored. The same loving impulse through which God reached out and created is impelled to reach out and draw back into itself all that has been lost.
- Love is not content until all is mended, with the final restoration of the cosmos (Rom. 8.21f). God's character drives God towards a goal, the goal of complete union, 'so that God may be all in all' (1 Cor. 15.28). Remarkably, God who is outside and beyond time enters time so that there may be a time when time matters no more. Love works in history and in our stories, and is eschatological in direction.
- Though God's love is directional and purposeful, it is not simply future-loaded. The persons of the Holy Trinity delight in their mutual dance as an end in itself. This is the 'pulsating dance of joy and love' of which Tim Keller speaks. Furthermore, the invitation to humanity to share in that dance is not merely an invitation to party in the hope of future blessing. It also welcomes us into a celebration that 'all is well' now, because we are with this God now.
- Many Christians are familiar with Andrei Rublev's

fifteenth-century Icon of the Holy Trinity, as it has almost become a visual cliché in today's church. Though icon painters (or writers as they are properly known) are not interested in perspective or realism of any kind, this icon gives the impression of a reverse perspective, drawing the viewer into this 'window into heaven'. In front of the table, facing forward, is a little door. Thus, the icon invites the viewer to enter the divine dance and emphasizes the fact that the Holy Trinity in its perichoretic dance welcomes the faithful at table, or we might say, at the ball!

- The act of spiritual direction models this 'invitation to the dance' through its offer of unconditional welcome and hospitality. It also reminds us that the primary locus of our encounter with God is that of communities, human communities engaging with the community of God's Holy Trinity. We are in this together.

We have noted that God may be known and acts unceasingly as the One who longs to be known. The Christian search for a vision of God is properly understood as a response to the divine invitation, and participation in the divine dance. This is sometimes reinforced by reference to the 'precious and very great promises' of God which enable us to 'become participants in the divine nature' (2 Peter 1.4). There is an immediate problem with this, because some mystical writers use it to suggest that the essential difference between divine nature and human nature is in the end broken down. We will need to return to this vexed question in Chapter 3 in discussing *theosis*.

The testimony of scripture and the Christian tradition as a whole makes it clear that there can be no ultimate merging of Creator and creatures, but that we participate in the divine nature by adoption and grace. We are dependent and unworthy, yet we are given a place which is not ours by right. The joy of the dance lies in knowing that the invitation is unconditional, and eternal. Unlike the doctrine of sovereignty, the metaphor of the divine dance focuses on our joyful creaturely response in the face of the generosity of a God who calls us to the dance.

The mystery of God's threeness

So far we have focused on ways in which we are drawn into the community of the divine dance, Three-in-One. Another part of the mystery of the nearness of God is that we can also, and often do, experience God in One-of-the-Three. In subsequent chapters we will think about such encounters with Jesus Christ as the human face of God, and with the Spirit, who brings the beyond near and wells up within us.

We also find ourselves engaging with God as the first person of the Trinity, the one whom we have already referred to metaphorically as Father. These moments of connection often come to us as a sense of the creativity of God, and relate to our experience of being made, of our smallness and insignificance, and a deep sense that we are held by God. In the context of spiritual direction, our task is to help those we accompany to interpret this experience as divine encounter.

In fact 'holding' is a key metaphor in one-to-one relationships and we'll say more about this at the end of the next chapter from a psychological perspective. For now though, it might be helpful to understand the first person of the Trinity as the 'holder' or 'upholder' of what happens in a direction session. The reader might like to associate this holding with the way the Father holds the Prodigal Son in Rembrandt's famous painting with, as Henri Nouwen points out in his book *The Return of the Prodigal Son,* two very differently shaped hands.

Unusually for someone of my personality type (more feeling than thinking), I most often come face to face with my creaturely status through reading popular science. The more I hear about genetics, or artificial intelligence, or fractals, the more I am struck by the intricacy of what is, and of who I am. It never fails to bring me back to the deep conviction of my childhood that the stuff of which I am made is neither random nor chance. The complexity of (my) matter takes me back to basics: I am the work of God, and in the language of Psalm 139, I am 'fearfully and wonderfully made' (verse 14). The first person of the Trinity is experienced by me as Maker, Creator, Scientist.

This may result in overwhelming wonder which leads to worship, or it may trigger a terror, that I am ultimately insignificant. In Chapter 4 we speak of times of descent into the inner darkness, where in Christ we discover that the places we fear most are often spiritual thresholds, places of redemption. Such moments of transformation also occur when we allow our fear of insignificance to become thresholds of encounter with the Creator God, and our smallness turns into the lightness of being held by the one who made us. For many, that has enabled us to think of the first person of the Trinity as both mothering and fathering us. Without falling into stereotypes of gender difference, we have learnt that one word (Father) does not encompass the whole of what we find in that person, who is also Sustainer, Guide, Friend and Companion. Broadening our language base at this point has the effect of creating new insights in the dynamic of our natural, or creation theology. We will come back to the theme of gender and God from time to time later in the book.

The beauty of God and our wonder

Medieval philosophers knew as well as we do that we cannot know God in essence, but only as God reaches out to us. They were, however, bold enough to suggest that God had a number of transcendentals, what we might call the deep character of God. Their suggested list of such transcendentals varied, but might include being, truth, goodness and beauty (Murphy, 1995, p. 213).

The Western Church has been very efficient at proclaiming a God whose truth is encapsulated in Christian doctrine, and at presenting a God whose goodness is reflected in the moral law. It has been neglectful of the idea of beauty as a way of meeting with God, for several reasons. Though Paul makes it clear in Romans 1.20 that God's 'eternal power and divine nature, invisible though they are, have been understood and seen through the things he has made', Reformation debates about grace and works silenced the voice of natural theology in Protestantism. In addition, our ambivalence about the value of the body dates back to early Christian thought, and punishing 'the flesh' has often been regarded as virtuous. Many commentators, reacting against artistic luxury, have treated the beauty of things as a distraction from the beauty of God.

Yet we know that all that is good has traces of the goodness that is God, and all that is true has traces of the truth that is God. Might we then not think that all that is beautiful has traces of the beauty that is God? 'The world is charged with the glory of God' as the Jesuit poet Gerard Manley Hopkins put it (1986, p. 27).

In the context of this chapter about a God who approaches, we suggest that beauty of all kinds is a God-given possibility, a symbolic visiting card, a glimpse that God is indeed passing by, coming very near. Clearly we would not want to construct a theology of the vision of God that made absolute connections between particular beautiful things or actions and the nearness of God. In the task of accompaniment, however, we are often called on to help those we direct to acknowledge or identify such things and actions as meeting points.

To illustrate this, I will tell a personal story. On 1 January 2006, I was in a playground in South Oxfordshire with part of my family, musing on profound struggles at work, when a green woodpecker flew straight across my path. Strangely, I sensed in that moment that God was saying that all would be well, an encouragement not to lose heart. The woodpecker did not cause me to hear God, and I do not understand the mechanics of what went on. All that I know is that over the years since then, whenever I have seen this bird, I have known God saying the same thing over and over.

Whenever I tell that story, people approach me with their own versions of a God who flashes past, giving glimpses of divine presence, favour and challenge. It should be noted here that by beauty, we do not mean a romantic ideal or something kitsch. Rather, beauty springs from a sense of shape, order, pattern, structure, harmony, proportion and splendour (see Eco, 2002, Ch. 1). Further, beauty is not static, and we experience beauty not just in the resolution of a discord, but in the discord itself. Beauty does not simply make us feel good in the presence of God. It also leads to challenge, development, transformation and enrichment.

One of the tasks of direction is to help directees to engage with the beauty of God. Wonder is not passive, and when we act out of our creative impulses, we are most likely to experience glimpses of divine presence. Because the artistic spirit is crushed in so many of us before we even leave school, it is not enough to suggest that a directee should 'take up music/poetry/painting'. Often, we need to work with people to help them discover that being created in the image and likeness of God means that we are gifted, able to build and rebuild, to 'co-create' the world with God. At a basic level, I often find myself nurturing the spiritual gift of appreciation, enabling others to see, hear, taste and touch the beauty around them.

The Word as sign of God's presence: revelation

Sometimes in practical theology we distinguish between ways of knowing God: through scripture, tradition, reason and experience. The sense of wonder that we have just written about is primarily experiential, though rooted in the biblical doctrines of creation and wisdom. The previous section on the divine dance might be located in the Christian tradition, built by seven or eight centuries of the Church's reflection on scripture.

The Anglican tradition out of which we both write is arguably both catholic and reformed. There are enough elements in it for both Catholics and Protestants to claim it for their own, and certainly sufficient grounds for calling it 'but halfly reformed' as the sixteenth-century Puritans did. But when Richard Hooker wrote his defining work on how Anglicans 'know' God – *On the Laws of Ecclesiastical Polity* in 1600 – he made it clear that scripture is primary: 'A full instruction in all things unto salvation necessary, the knowledge whereof man by nature could not otherwise in this life attain unto …' (1907, Vol. I, p. 279).

In the light of this, we move in this section to underline the fact that God is revealed to us formally, first in the Holy Scriptures and then also through the sacraments, themselves derived from the scriptural witness.

And this is the central point, that the Bible is not best understood as a repository of infallible truth. It is God's tool or instrument of repeated and insistent self-introduction. It is the language of dialogue between me, us, others and God. It is human speech and it is divine speech. God is not embedded in the words but in the process of the conversation. God is made known through human stories with which the divine intention intersects and engages. We will say much more of this in Chapter 6.

Understanding the Scriptures in this way ought to set us free from futile debates about how reliable the Bible is. Taking our guide from 2 Timothy 3.16, we recognize that scripture is inspired by God and *useful* to us. It is reliable because through it God meets us, welcomes us, challenges us and if we allow it, transforms us. What one might call spiritual readings of scripture (*Lectio Divina,* the Ignatian Spiritual Exercises, Base Christian Community practice) are marked out by the expectation that the reader will be liberated, directed, guided into new life as a result.

This means that in the shared journey of spiritual direction, the director may not use the Scriptures to control the person they are directing, as if they possessed some magical power and authority as a result of fuller theological or doctrinal understanding of 'what the Scriptures actually mean'. Our task with respect to the Scriptures is

- to direct those we accompany to the Word, in the confidence that in them, God seeks to approach, to talk and to listen;
- to 'eat' the Scriptures, using the vivid language of Ezekiel 3 and Revelation 10, hinting at the need to eat slowly/digest, to eat up and not be selective, to eat and be fed; and
- to 'be read' by them. Malcolm Guite in his sonnet 'The Lectern' says that: 'God's strange grace, red as these ribbons, red/ As your own blood when reading reads you here/ And pierces joint and marrow' (2012, loc. 358). We do not possess the truth of the Scriptures; through them, when we read them well, God not only meets us but lays hold of us, shakes us, even consumes us. Guite's allusion in the poem is to Hebrews 4.12f and the painful laying bare which happens in the presence of the living God.

So we expect to meet God, to discern the presence of God, when we engage with the Scriptures. That encounter is an invitation to remain and rest in the presence of God, certainly, but it is more. It is an invitation to become participants or actors in the divine story. Sam Wells builds on Tom Wright's understanding of the divine drama of salvation revealed in the Bible and played out in five acts – the five acts being creation, Israel, Jesus, the Church and finally the eschaton (2004, pp.53-4 – we will look at Wells' work here in more detail in Chapter 6). Christians are in the fourth act in which we are active and improvising participants in the mission of God. This truth is a useful counterfoil to the idea that when we read the Scriptures, we are passive subjects on whom God works. God certainly does work on us when God meets us, but we also join in working with God, active participants who have value, responsibility and shared ownership of the journey of faith.

The Bible is a door into a world of infinite Kingdom possibilities, and one of the key tasks of spiritual accompaniment is to lead people to that door, and help them open it for themselves, in one-to-one encounters, but also in public liturgical reading and in preaching and in the very act of direction itself.

'Other' sacraments as signs of God's presence: revelation

There is a tiresome and fruitless debate about how many sacraments there are, and I favour the Orthodox view that there are sacraments or holy mysteries, and then there are sacramentals. All of them are based on Christ the Great Sacrament, himself the complete outward and visible sign of God's grace and presence for us which is well illustrated by the title of Edward Schillebeeckx's classic *Christ the Sacrament of the Encounter with God* (1987).

The argument is a simple one: the Church is given the sacraments so that in them we may encounter Christ. In encountering Christ, we encounter the whole Godhead. It has been a sadness in my directing role to meet so many Christians for whom the Church is a stumbling block rather than a means of revelation. A crucial part of the directing task must be to reintroduce people to the possibility that God may be revealed to us, formally and institutionally, even by a fractured and often ungodly Church:

Just as Christ through his risen body acts invisibly in the world, he acts visibly in and through his earthly body, the Church, in such a way that the sacraments are the personal saving acts of Christ realized as institutional acts in the Church. (Schillebeeckx, 1987, loc. 694)

As we can agree that there are at least two (key) sacraments, let us consider briefly how Baptism and Holy Communion become for us, in the Church, signs of the revealed presence of God, means of encounter, and invitations into divine hospitality.

Baptism is given to us as the 'welcome home' of the prodigal (generous) Father to the prodigal (wasteful) son. Just as in the biblical narrative, when the son comes to the father only to find the father coming to him, so in the sacramental act we come seeking God only to discover that God has come to seek us. There is an act of grace, an unconditional welcoming in; there is a concrete context, the Church, which acts out the hospitality of God at the core of its being: one of the core marks of the Church. And there is a formal character to the act: that which is done is really done. We have been met by God and brought home.

In the same vein in Holy Communion, the welcome home includes an invitation to the table. We come to receive Christ through word, bread and wine, and find that Christ has given himself to us. There is another act of grace, an unconditional feeding with all that we need; there is a concrete context, the Church, which takes its part in giving all that we need. And again there is a formal character to the act: the one who invites us to the feast sits at the table with us. God does not depart as we arrive. In some sense, there is a real presence, and with that proviso, Protestants and Catholics might just agree!

In our post-romantic, individualized culture, we seek the proof of everything in the way it feels to us. The burden of proof even in Christian journeys so often lays heavy on the disciple. If I do not know it, how can it be true? So the formal assurance that a key part of the knowability of God lies outside us, formally in the community of grace (the Church), is fundamental to healthy spiritual growth. It does not, after all, depend wholly on me, or even on one other individual (the soul friend). It is given to us in a rich and diverse community of the faithful against which the gates of hell and despair will not prevail.

The essence of God

Before we move on to discuss ways in which we communicate with our knowable and approachable God, we need to pause briefly and ask whether our experience of this God is reliable and essentially true. Though as a practical theologian and spiritual director I often find myself impatient with the abstract or esoteric nature of this question, I am aware that on it hangs the possibility of spiritual assurance and the confidence that we are not deceiving ourselves or being deceived by God. As Frances Young puts it, 'Job couldn't let God be God, but trapped God in his questions, until confronted with the divine reality' (2011, p. 385).

The first question is whether what we know about God is everything that can be known. The answer is a quick and simple No: 'Now I know only in part; then I will know fully, even as I have been fully known' (1 Cor. 13.12). This is embedded in the doctrine of transcendence, the beyond-ness of God which means that God cannot be captured or confined by our experiences. Put differently, if we knew everything that could be known about God, then God would be contained in our knowing, an object observed, and so would cease to be God.

Less trivially, the second question is whether what we know about God is consonant with the being or essential nature of God. It is possible to conceive of the gods playing games with us, full of deceit and trickery. Greek mythology gives us Dolos, the lying spirit born of Gaia and Aether, carried across into

Roman texts as Mendacius, the mendacious spirit! At a more philosophical level, the discussion about self and non-self in Upanishadic and Theravada Buddhist theology raises the same question in a more sophisticated way: does ultimate reality bear any resemblance to life as we experience it on this earth?

In the fourth century, a group of theologians who came to be known as the Cappadocian Fathers[6] worked on the doctrine of the Trinity, and made an important distinction between the immanent Trinity (God as God is in Godself) and the economic Trinity (God as God comes to be known through activity in the cosmos). Put simply, we only know God in and through the actions of God (God is a verb), but those actions are entirely consistent with the inner nature of God. In other words, though we will not know in this life all or even most that there is to be known about God, what we know comes from God's desire to make God's own true essence available to us, that we may be drawn into the Godhead. The banquet matches the promise on the invitation.

There are two cautions here. The first is that though it is right and proper to speak aloud about God and who we conceive God to be, we must never speak in such a way that we mistake the part that we know for the 'whole of God', or speak arrogantly, as if our knowledge contained God in some way. Directors need to warn themselves against this kind of spiritual arrogance too.

The second is that language is culturally limited. In English, it's hard to talk about God without using the language of gender. When I worked in South Africa, where language is less gendered, I was set free for a while from an angst about making God masculine. The deeply gendered structures of English simply remind us of what a patriarchal tradition we have inherited. God is not part of that

---

6 Basil of Caesarea (330–79), his brother Gregory of Nyssa (335–c. 395) and Gregory of Nazianzen (329–89), named Cappadocian because they came from the region of Cappadocia, now in Turkey. We have already mentioned the second Gregory in talking about the 'divine dance' earlier in the chapter.

tradition, and we do the gospel (and God) a grave disservice if we allow God to be culturally and traditionally bound. God is neither human, nor male, nor female, but carefully used human language with its female and male images may help us humbly to begin to describe our experiences of God.

The divine conversation

Love intends a relationship with all that it creates, as we said earlier. Though we have to be careful about talking of God as if God were human, the best analogy for the communication on which our relationship with God depends is the analogy of conversation. Prayer is best described as our languages of communication with God, and forms of prayer as the grammar and syntax of communication.

If God communicates with us through scripture and the sacraments, through tradition, reason and experience, then the dialogic nature of our relationship with God means that the same is true of us. There are indeed different 'languages' with which we might speak to God and about God. It is probably not helpful, however, to divide prayer up into those categories. More useful is the idea that in the spirit of narrative or story-telling theology, we address God in two ways: in the language God is currently using with us; and in the language of our own current experience. In this way, we show respect to God by listening to the different ways in which God chooses to speak to us on a particular occasion (scripture, liturgy, nature, reason, conscience and so on) and by responding in like vein.

When we respond in this range of languages made available to us in the Christian tradition, we respond out of our own life experience and also out of our own God-experience. It is this dynamic that makes the role and task of spiritual direction both fascinating and tricky. There are four forces at work:

1. God as God is, in essence, unknowable yet reaching out to be known.
2. God as I experience God: God revealed to me.
3. My life circumstances, the raw material and reflection on that material over time.
4. The interplay between God and how I know God and how I think God is implicated in the joys and sorrows, the blessings and curses, the causes and effects that shape my life.

In the interplay between these four forces, we observe both the uniqueness of the individual and the consistency of God. God as described in this chapter is consistently the one who is, who longs for encounter with the creation and who works at being known, who is always near/here,[7] who invites us into full participation in the hospitality of the Godhead.

The process of spiritual direction operates within this interplay of forces. A key role of the director is to inhabit that complex and sometimes confusing space with the one being directed, enabling creative engagement. In the face of divine consistency in self-giving without limits, our *primary* task is to invite a responsive consistency on the part of the person we are accompanying (and to model that same consistency in our lives and directing). The difference for us is that human consistency lies not in always being the same, but always being true to the people we are. It is the consistency of integrity and of rigorous honesty, an ability to pour ourselves out in the presence of a God who comes without reserve. It demands a recognition that God is big enough to take the whole of my life into the divine embrace.

There has been in recent years a plethora of writing in

---

7 Or as Philip Roderick, founder of Contemplative Fire (https://contemplativefire.org/) has put it following Thomas Merton: 'Now/here', i.e. both present (here and now) and absent (nowhere).

evangelical circles about the apparent inability of evangelical Christians to lament, poignantly underlined by Stephen Torr in writing about his mother's death: 'So, what does one do in the wreckage of the aftermath? How does one think about, talk about and, most importantly, talk to a God who it was believed could do something but actually seemed absent at the most crucial moments?' (2013, p. 107f). The case of evil and suffering is not the only one that demands rigorous integrity in our relationship with a God who comes, but it sharpens the discussion. If we cannot express to God our confusion, our doubt, our anger and rage in language and liturgy appropriate to those intense passions, then all participation in the divine conversation becomes ultimately meaningless. If all we can say to God is that 'it's all OK, thanks', then God is the ultimate irrelevance.

In the course of writing this chapter, living in a former mining village in South Derbyshire, we've had far more 'spiritual' conversations than we expected with our new neighbours. A recent one on the pavement went something like this:

'So you're a priest?'

'Yes.'

'I've lost my faith. Can I talk to you?'

'Of course you can. Come round whenever you're ready.'

'I've got mental health problems. You won't judge me because I've lost my faith, will you?'

'No. Of course not.'

Apart from a deep unease and sadness that the institutional Church seems better known for its ability to judge than its ability to listen, I was struck by the way in which this seemed to be the beginning of another 'divine conversation'. Neither cataphatic (she didn't voice any actual words of prayer) nor apophatic (no contented silence here), it seemed rather to be an indirect and mediated conversation in which God had become the silent partner, somewhere hazily on the edges. Certainly

God is beyond her reach at the moment, but it was remarkable how easily she used me, the 'professional Christian', as an intermediary. It was not that she needed me, but perhaps this was the beginning of a journey of mediated prayer.

It was a moment fraught with possibility and with danger. The possibility is that of glimpsing an ever-present God, straining towards us in love. The danger is that the intermediary – me in this case but the director or companion in general – acts *in loco Dei* or *in loco parentis,* and supplements or supplants the need for encounter with the true and living God.

Reflection and questions

- How do you relate to the metaphor of God's constant approach and nearness – God as a verb, as flow? As you think about ways in which you have encountered God, write (or draw, paint, sculpt etc.) a personal reflection on those encounters as part of the divine dance.

- The Church sometimes seems to be polarized between those who find God in the Scriptures, and those for whom the sacraments are key. Think of the range of ways in which God has been made known to you, and attempt to construct a personal theology of revelation which is less polarized.

- List your preferred languages of conversation with God, and note whether there are any significant ways of communicating with God with which you struggle. How might you journey with someone whose spiritual languages are different to yours?

- What impact does suffering and evil have on your understanding of the nature and presence of God? Note ways in which you (and perhaps others with whom you worship or work) experience and encounter God in the midst of life's struggles. In what ways does this chapter help to broaden or clarify that experience of God?

- How might your responses to any of the above questions affect your being directed as a disciple of Christ or in your directing of others?

2

The Human Person in Companionship

In the introductory chapter we indicated that the subject of this chapter is people themselves (technically we will be discussing theological anthropology). There are several questions we will explore such as: who are these two human beings sitting together in a room with each other, discerning the movement of God among them? How much or little might we expect of them, both as individuals, as Christian community and as part of the human race? What is the nature of the journey that in fact both are on in different ways? What effect might the gender and sexuality of the persons involved have on their relationship, if any? And to conclude we will look at what light other disciplines, especially psychology, can throw on spiritual companionship.

John Donne (1573-1631) was sitting in his study near St Paul's Cathedral in London when he heard the bell tolling for a funeral. He wrote a meditation on his experience which included the classic line 'no man [sic] is an island'. In the context of the end of life he recognizes that we are all connected, that none of us is ever alone and entirely disconnected – however lonely that death might have been. In addition, the death of anyone diminishes us all – and we will all meet that same fate and thus we are all part of a whole. So here is a good place to start, with the two people sitting in a room with the door closed, discerning the movement of God. Neither of them prays entirely alone, but more importantly neither of them exists alone and this basic fact of their communitarian existence is, at least in part, what drives them together and makes their relationship necessary.

THE HUMAN PERSON IN COMPANIONSHIP

The image of God in humanity and spiritual direction

The human being is a 'being-in-communion'. In the western world for the last few hundred years we have emphasized the importance of the individual over the community and the dictum, coined by René Descartes (1596-1650), 'I think therefore I am' has rather reigned over our lives. We have often come to think of ourselves as autonomous individuals and such thinking has infected the Church and Christians too (without us realizing it of course). For instance, if I have a direct 'personal relationship with Jesus' as it is sometimes termed, which is a good thing in itself, then I might not see the need to sit with another to discern the activity of God in my life and my prayer.

Our African sisters and brothers have taught us an important lesson here as they dance to a different drum – the beat of 'I am because we are' or the idea of Ubuntu (in isiZulu) or Utu (in Kiswahili). That is, none of us exists, as Donne knew, without the community, the whole. Yet even here the individual can become totally subsumed in the community or the community can define itself antagonistically against other communities that are different. So while there are advantages and disadvantages to both approaches, neither is 'ideal'. It is easy to romanticize either way of thinking, so we need to set the importance of *both* the individual *and* the community in the context of the theology of the creation of human beings in the 'image of God', *imago Dei* (Gen. 1.27). Stanley Grenz puts this well in interacting with the work of the Orthodox theologian John Zizioulas: first 'there is no true being without communion', so that 'communion is an ontological category'. And second, communion that does not originate from a concrete and free person and does not lead to concrete and free persons 'is not an "image" of the being of God'. In short: 'The person cannot exist without communion; but every form of communion which denies or suppresses the person, is inadmissible' (2001, pp. 52-3).

Here is a very powerful argument for the importance of spiritual direction and also its efficacy – why it 'works'. The spiritual being of one person is being attended to by both that person and another in the presence of the three persons of the One God. What better setting might illustrate 'being-in-communion'? Let's see if we can underline this argument still further. We have mentioned the *imago Dei* and many books have been written on what it means to be created in God's image so we'll need to summarize as succinctly as we can here.

First we note that it is both males and females *together* that represent God's image in Genesis, especially in the plural repetition in the second half of the verse and in the second creation story in the garden (we will return to the theme of gender later in the chapter). Thus we might suggest that the creation of humanity is a plurality in unity rather than a creation of discrete entities who are then invited to relate. On the side of the Creator there is even a hint, the scholars tell us at this early stage in the Bible, of some plurality in God which is being mirrored in the bringing into being of plural humanity in the first Hebrew creation narrative. Christians have come to understand God as community, as we noted in the previous chapter – three persons in ever-loving relationships. Therefore, if God is one community while being three distinct persons and we are made in God's image then we are made for community too and hence meeting with another in the presence of the Triune God connects us deeply to our formation as beings-in-communion. So the image of God in people is *the inherent capacity for relationship* – with God, with other human beings and with creation.

Second, as Zizioulas and Grenz pointed out, the image of God also has to do with the 'concrete and free person' who has the ability to make choices, whether for good or ill. God creates the world out of the overflow of love which exists in God – God freely and joyfully creates. God has no 'need' to create others to love and yet chooses to do so from the abundant overflow of love. So it is with humanity, each one has a moment by moment choice to make around moving towards or away from the love that is sourced ultimately in God.

So finally, and summing up the meaning of *imago Dei* for us, there is an 'analogy of being' between humans and God – a likeness in how humans are created that unites them with God at the very core of their being. They are mysteriously connected in ways that are not quite the same for other creatures, they are the pinnacle of creation and those who are given responsibility for creation. Humans have the capacity to desire God and become united with God – in their very being. This, as we have noted, is the goal of the spiritual direction relationship. All of which places God at the centre of created existence as pure gift, and means humans are 'eccentric' to that – to coin a phrase of David Kelsey in *Eccentric Existence*. What Kelsey means is that our propensity, as we shall see, is to place ourselves at the centre of existence. Biblical faith always places God at the centre and human beings peripheral or eccentric to that centre.

So here we have some clues to a conundrum I regularly come across when companioning others. Without going into any detail, one of my directees was extremely grateful for the change that had occurred in the few years we had been meeting. I was profusely thanked for my contribution to a renewed spiritual life. I was tempted to deflect the thanks and to say, rather too piously: 'Well, we must give thanks to God – this is all God's work in you'. But I had to admit if I hadn't been available, ready to meet and be present to the activity of God in the directee the transformation that had occurred simply wouldn't have. It is never all about the director or all about God, it is about beings-in-communion where, when the door is closed and safe space is created, transformational divine – human cooperation can take place.

The dark side: disordered desire as sin

So much for our starting point in creation and if only it were so easy. Something has gone horribly wrong with humanity as we all know – the question which exercises theologians at this point is how wrong it has actually gone. Some believe that human rebellion against God has obliterated the original image within us – the capacity for relationship, for choosing right, for being connected to God deep, deep down inside us. Others reject this as far too pessimistic a view which is simply not commensurate with the complete mixture that human beings are: capable of amazing works of beauty, truth and goodness as well as of despicable acts of cruelty, spite and deep darkness.

This is not the place to sort these arguments out, yet in a chapter on Christian anthropology in spiritual direction we cannot not deal with the dark side of being human. Again many bottles of ink have been used up over this question, but what could we usefully say here that is relevant for our subject? We'll need to address the question of sin and what it is (or is not). And it's worth saying straightaway a mistake we could make is to under- or over-estimate the importance of the reality of 'sin' in human life. I believe our starting point is always best chosen from what *is* working well, what *is* right, what *is* good. This is the principle behind what we might call the first rule of prayer for any beginner: 'Pray as you can, not as you can't.' Once we have established an appreciative 'bridgehead' then we have permission to engage with deeper, darker issues that arise as we set out with courage having a go with what we can do.

There are many definitions of sin: falling short (Rom. 3.23); breaking the Ten Commandments (Luke 18.20); living an unjust life (Luke 18.22) to name a few. To return to Genesis there are two related aspects of sin that are particularly relevant to the spiritual guidance task. What seems to be being portrayed in the whole of Genesis 1—11 (we should never just stick to Genesis

3 alone), culminating in the tower of Babel, is a rejection of the fundamental eccentricity of humans to life and relationships on our planet. God is at the centre of the created order and while humanity might be the pinnacle of creation we are still just mortal creatures who are gifted breath and life and time on this earth out of the abundance of the love of God. We, it seems from generation to generation, reject this reality and place ourselves at the centre of our lives, denying that all is gift from the overflow of abundant love. And yet we still, deep down somewhere, desire relationship, even relationship with God (perhaps I am betraying my position on how far God's image is broken in us!) – even if that is totally focused on us and our ability to build a tower and somehow become equal to God out of our own resources (Gen. 11).

I find a helpful way of thinking about sin (which takes it utterly seriously, but avoids the moralistic baggage that often comes with the way the word has been used in our culture) is as 'disordered desire'. This is not a new idea, it can be traced way back to the desert Fathers and Mothers in the fourth century who retreated into their remote desert cells to deliberately face their dark side head on, following of course Jesus' example (Luke 4.1–13; for further reading on this subject see Angela Tilby, *The Seven Deadly Sins*). It is in fact the origin of the development of the classic seven 'deadly sins' of pride, greed, lust, envy, gluttony, wrath and sloth. If you get underneath these particular sins you can see the root of them is desiring too much (gluttony), desiring in the other direction from God (pride) or even not desiring enough (sloth).

A more contemporary word for this state within the human condition is addiction. We are desiring beings and made so by God, as we have seen. This is the basis of the huge multi-billion-dollar worldwide advertising industry and the way most country's economies are run based on the theory of consumer capitalism. Advertisers appeal to our basic desires, which is not in itself a bad thing – and it really works! Think about it. We all need food, we are biologically programmed to desire it and without it we die. However, very few of us, especially after midlife when our metabolism slows down, can afford to fully obey our desire and satisfy our hunger all the time, therefore eating what we like when we like. Yet every coffee house we go into will want to sell us 'a pastry with that, madam?'

Unfortunately, disordered desire can go in all sorts of directions. Yes of course mind-altering drugs are highly addictive as are, for some, activities like looking at pornography. Then there are more mundane activities such as gambling and alcohol which can easily take us over. But anything can be addictive and we are all to a greater or lesser extent addicted to all sorts of things including basics like food and mobile phones. There is no escape, no looking down on anyone else saying 'Thank God, I am not like this one' (Luke 18.11). Even work and our Christian ministry can be addictive if it is based on our 'need to be needed'. It will then begin to rule over us and we lose our sense of self in an ever-busier flurry of activity that is far from God's desires for us.

Prayer, especially contemplative or silent prayer, addresses this basic disorientation of our lives. The theologian Sarah Coakley has written brilliantly on this subject (*God, Sexuality and the Self*). She, like Tilby, also takes her cue from Evagrius Ponticus (who was related to those desert Fathers in the fourth century) since he wrote that a theologian 'is one whose [contemplative] prayer is true' (which of course opens the possibility of any praying person being a theologian!). Many of the teachers of this apophatic or negative way of prayer in silence show that it is a path that goes through purgation (a kind of 'cleansing' of the egotistical, addicted self that gets in the way of God) and illumination before reaching union with God. As Coakley states:

the very act of contemplation – repeated, lived, embodied, suffered – is an act that, by grace, and over time, inculcates mental patterns of 'un-mastery', welcomes the dark realm of the unconscious, opens up radical attention to the 'other', and instigates an acute awareness of the messy entanglement of sexual desires and desire for God. (2013, p. 43)

In silent contemplation then God takes God's rightful place, as at the beginning described in Genesis – as that 'without which there would be nothing at all' (p. 44). God sustains all being and in contemplation human powers fall away so that we become known by God rather than just seeking to know God in prayer (p. 45). We discover true desire as a 'naked intent towards God' as the medieval author of *The Cloud of Unknowing* puts it. Then something shifts in the silence of prayer such that we can receive the original gift once again and place God at the centre of our lives within creation. Prayer moves from being all about us to being all about God.

It is no surprise then that two of the hardest things in my experience to maintain in a spiritual direction relationship are a) silence and b) a focus on God as centre, ground, giver and sustainer of all things. They are no doubt intimately related. Silence takes many forms, some of which are quite 'awkward' and difficult, but the kind of silence we are cultivating in direction is a contemplative one where all the 'beings' in the room are free to let each other be and at the same time become. When such silence is possible and maintained, God's presence and movement at the centre are more easily discerned. Once again this is why spiritual companionship is so vital. Where else is a somewhat hidden hour set aside with, let us say it, an intimate other to lift our disorderly desires into the light and realign them with God's desires for us?

Liberation, interior freedom and the holistic view of persons

Let us return for a moment to the idea of 'concrete and free persons', focusing appropriately on the individual, remembering now that the human subject is always a being-in-communion. The path of purgation, illumination and union, however unique and convoluted it might be for each person who travels it, is a path, we believe, of liberation. There is an old rabbinical saying that goes something like this. At the last judgement God will not ask me why I was not more like Moses, or Elijah or Jeremiah. God will simply ask why I was not more like Nigel.

Thomas Merton (1915–68) often wrote about the path of spiritual becoming as a journey to the 'true self'. We have seen hints of this possibility already in this chapter. Thus the journey to union which we might understand as coming to a consummate fruition in seeing face to face at the end of time (Rev. 22.4) is a gradual letting go of our egocentric 'false selves'. In doing so we discover our true self which is found in relationships where God is at the centre. This true self does not have a separate existence and cannot be isolated, or put under a microscope as it were. Nevertheless it is a concrete reality which can be experienced in all its fullness and it is free, liberated, unique, true to itself and the way the Creator meant it to be.

My experience of directing others is often one of watching the chains and shackles of upbringing, disordered desire, unhelpful voices, dysfunctional religion and many other things fall away from a person. In this process it is as if they become 'bigger'. I am reminded of the word *Mahātmā*, applied as it was to Mohandas K. Gandhi (1869–1948), which means 'great soul'. This visible growth affects the whole person. Often it changes the way a face looks, people begin to wear different clothes, project their anxieties less and simply have a new spring in their step.

Which brings us to an assumption about the 'holistic'

nature of persons we have been working with until now, but which probably needs spelling out in this chapter. People are whole selves, just as their 'self' is only found in communion, in relationship so it is with all the parts that make up a person. We often refer, as the Bible does too, to a person's body, soul, spirit, mind, heart, strength, among other possible ways of regarding the human person. Once again, we haven't the space here to go in to a long discussion of how these concepts are defined and whether the soul can be understood separately to the body or what it is of a human person that is continuous through death to the resurrected life. Nevertheless, in this mortal life, treating people as holistic beings, where all the parts that make them up are understood simply as *aspects* of their whole, seems sensible, has biblical warrant and is true to experience.

If this is the case then prayer encompasses the whole self which perhaps most importantly of all in the western world involves the *body* and the *heart*. It is fair to say that we have become alienated from our bodies in the West. My own journey has been one of moving out of my head, my mind, to praying in an embodied way, paying attention to body posture in prayer and noticing the minute itches and ticks that come and go in my body as potential distractions. And then in illumination it is said that prayer moves from originating in the head (from my effort to make it happen as we have seen) to the heart where it is gifted to us, since God dwells there. From this place at the centre the whole person is affected by the liberation that occurs.

The implication of a holistic approach to the human person in spiritual direction is therefore that nothing in the life of the directee is outside of any attention the directee and the director might pay to it. Of course there are boundaries or edges to how spiritual direction might address such things (we are not counsellors or gym instructors for example), but if God is to be at the centre of the true self then everything matters. Everything that occurs in body, mind, and spirit can be a starting point down through which the presence and movement of God can be discerned. Knowing this as a director helps me in that brief moment of anxiety at the start of a session when I wonder, 'What will *N* bring today and will I be able to hold it and work with it effectively?'

Gender and sexuality

Having spoken of the body in spiritual direction it is not a big step to address questions of gender and sexuality, from which there should be no escape in thinking about good practice in spiritual companionship. And yet for a myriad of reasons it is a subject we often shy away from.

Human beings are gendered sexual beings on a continuum – an entity which is a complex mixture of biology, identity, gender and sexuality (for further reading on this see Adrian Thatcher, *God, Sex and Gender*). Every directee and every director there ever was or will be is a gendered sexual being. It matters not whether the two people meeting together are of the same sex or the opposite, the question of gender and sexuality will always be present, even if it is deep in the unconscious of the relationship that is forming. As we have already noted, our gendered diversity as beings-in-communion is part of the image of God, the way God has created us. It is a good thing, to be treasured and utilized for more good.

One of the experiences that has taught me most about sexuality is becoming good friends with a British religious sister whom I met many years ago while in Tanzania (she has since died). Despite (or perhaps because of) being well into the second half of her life and a celibate religious sister, it seemed to me that she was able to use her sexuality to gain large amounts of leverage in what was a mainly patriarchal society. It was a marvel to watch her in action or listen to her stories of how doors seemed to open up for her and her alone when something 'simply had to be done'. I think this was because her lifelong spiritual practice had helped her to 'master' her sexuality, or, to put it another way, that through prayer her sexuality had found its most creative place in her life.

Armed with this experience, reading the theologian Sarah Coakley on prayer, gender and sexuality makes so much more sense. For Coakley, the divinely ordered person places the contemplative approach to both prayer and the world as the 'primary ascetical submission to the divine demanded by revelation'. Thus the 'whole self (intellect, will, memory, imagination, feeling, bodiliness)' becomes attentively open to 'the reality of God and of the creation' (2013, p. 88). In this way questions of sex and gender become properly ordered within the category of *desire* since 'divine desire purgatively reforms human desire' (p. 59).

There is therefore nothing to fear about gender or sexuality in the spiritual guidance relationship – and the same goes for any other identity markers in director or directee such as race or disability. What is required is an open, contemplative, inquiring stance when questions of gender and sexuality arise in either directee or director. And, it goes without saying also in the supervisory relationship that every director requires.

Inter-disciplinary approaches to the person in spiritual direction

We have largely stayed with theological approaches to the human person until this point, not least because we want to maintain the centrality of God to what is happening in the spiritual direction room. It is now time to broaden this out and examine what other disciplines might bring to understanding people and especially close one-to-one relationships.

We could draw on many scholarly discourses when thinking

about human beings – philosophy, biology, psychology, sociology and even cultural anthropology. We have briefly touched on some philosophical aspects of the human being such as the existence of the soul. We might usefully explore the relationship between human brains and religious experience. That is, is a propensity for religion 'hard-wired' in our biological make-up? However, for our practical purposes in this book on spiritual companionship, we will spend the major part of this section interacting with insights from the psychology of the human person.

First a word about the legitimacy of this exercise in theology. Without making a full apology for drawing on other disciplines in practical theology here, let us state a few important points. If God is the creator and sustainer of all that 'is' then social-scientific disciplines such as psychology are part of that creation. They are truth-seeking just as much as theology is. Of course they can be used to the detriment of humanity as some of the history of the twentieth century shows, but in general they are describing what 'is' in human beings for the purposes of using that information for the good of all. Why would we not as Christians therefore take critical account of the truths revealed through disciplines such as psychology? Perhaps the key word here is 'critical' as we do not take anything for granted, but place our inter-disciplinary learning in dialogue with both theology and experience.

There are two main ways in which psychology interacts with our subject. The first is in thinking about the praying subject – the individual human being – and the second is describing the inter-personal dynamics between director and directee.

Psychological insights into the praying subject

Spiritual directors need to be familiar with this area since it is very popular in describing the personality type preferences of individuals and it is claimed that there is some kind of relationship between personality type and preferred styles of prayer and spirituality. We might, by the way, note the same sort of relationship between personality preferences and the different spiritual traditions – Benedictine, Dominican, Ignatian, Carmelite, etc.

A highly influential school among Christians in recent times has been the Myers-Briggs Type Indicator (MBTI) which is based on the psychology of Carl Jung (1875–1961). Jung was a disciple of Sigmund Freud (1856–1939), but broke away from him, not least around questions of the efficacy of religion. Another is the Enneagram, which is also a personality type indicator and has a much more complex history which it is claimed goes back to ancient times (websites on both approaches say much more). The first critical point to make is that I think it is best to understand these and other personality type indicators as *tools* for understanding more about ourselves (since the spiritual journey is about revealing our 'true self' as we have seen). However, all tools have their limits. It is no good trying to use a hammer on a screw, or a hacksaw designed for cutting metal on a wooden plank.

These tools reveal much and explain much about ourselves and when we first come across them it often seems like a revelation – how could someone know that much about us? Yet we believe it is a mistake to limit ourselves to their description of us since our own persons are much more complex. Let us take the example of MBTI as a short case study in critical thinking about the use of such psychological tools, which I will relate to my own experience of it.

MBTI divides all people universally into sixteen personality types around four sets of polarities in each one's personality (which are all given letters), the most memorable of which is the extraversion (E)–introversion (I) continuum. To describe it rather crudely, extraverts prefer to gain their energy from relating externally to other people, while introverts are energized preferably from within, in their own company.

It is not unusual for people, having taken the MBTI test and been given their four letters, to begin to claim that, for instance, 'I am ISFP' and then they ask what you are! This despite all the MBTI sessions I have been on where the trainers emphasize that the letters are about your ego personality *preferences*, just as we have preference for writing with our right or left hand and it is harder to write with the other. So in my case it was extremely helpful when starting out in ministry to realize I have a preference for introversion, which didn't mean I am stuck with just doing interior things. Only that I needed to recognize that after some extraverted activity such as leading worship or conducting a funeral I needed some recovery time, as my energy was drained. Thus, just as I am not entirely my DNA, or my family tree, or my job, or my gender, neither am I my MBTI profile. To return to the theme of this chapter I am made up of many things all of which create my being-in-communion.

And there is more to Jung's psychological theory than is described by the MBTI ego preferences which is also often missed by people being introduced to the ideas for the first time. Jung's theory goes something like what follows here (there are many more erudite books that can explain it much better, this is simply a summary – see e.g. Christopher Bryant, *Jung and the Christian Way*).

We are given our ego preferences, generally they don't change throughout our lives, and sure enough mine haven't. However, we spend the first half of our lives living them out – working with them if you like, establishing ourselves and our place in the world. The effect of this, by the age of around 35–45, is that they have created an inevitable and necessary 'shadow' which consists of their opposites at the other end of the continuum. That shadow then begins to assert itself in our personality – it kind of takes on a life of its own and wants to be noticed, but coming as it does from the unconscious we tend to ignore or repress it. This in my case made me get angry for very little reason as I entered what I came to call my 'mid-life transition' (it wasn't that much of a 'crisis' for me). Jung states that the task of the second half of life is to integrate the shadow with the ego to create what he calls the 'individuated' self. This self is a rounded and whole person which has to be related, in my opinion, to the 'true self' of Merton and others; one of the goals of the spiritual journey, as we have noted. This is the basis of much of the work of the Franciscan spiritual writer Richard Rohr, especially in his book *Falling Upward*.

All this has been true to my own experience as the spiritual journey I have been taken on since my late thirties has helped me move towards my integrated or true self. I look forward to and even enjoy extraverted activity in the moment now, having done this work. However, it isn't some sort of magic which removes altogether episodes of anger, for instance, and it is constant hard work in co-operation with God (and a good spiritual director of course!).

So for me, I am happy to work with Jungian psychological theory, as it fits my experience and I can connect it to the long spiritual tradition. However, I hope you can see I do not do this uncritically and recognize the limits that it has as a tool to help on the journey.

There are other ways to approach the human person from a psychological perspective. There is not too much space to describe them here, but mention should be made of some. The existence of the unconscious, while contentious for some, makes perfect sense to me and why we should take our dreams and waking thoughts seriously in both prayer and spiritual direction. The stages of human development delineated by Erik Erikson (1902–94), related as they are to James Fowler's faith development theories (*Stages of Faith*), are good background to some of the transitions that directees will face. In addition, when thinking about growth Joanna Collicutt has an important work on the psychology of Christian formation (*The Psychology of Christian Character Formation*). Finally, I have recently engaged with object relations theory from Melanie Klein (1882–1960), not least because she describes how the infant self is created in relationship to the mother in the first few months of life. The normal movement in an infant is from experiencing plenty in the 'good breast' and scarcity in the 'bad breast', which is eventually resolved in discovering a 'good enough' mother. These early experiences have important effects on the person as they mature in relation to how they love, hate and find the 'good enough' in other people.

Interpersonal psychodynamics in spiritual direction

Speaking of good enough I believe there is a 'minimum knowledge base' in the psychology of one-to-one relationships that spiritual guides require. Directors who come from counselling or other therapeutic backgrounds will be much more familiar with terms like projection, introjection, transference and counter-transference from the psychological field. It is not our place to describe them in detail here as there is ample literature available (e.g. Sue Pickering, *Spiritual Direction*, especially Chapters 4 and 5). What is notable is the concrete shape these effects give to the 'space between' two people. As we come to the conclusion of this chapter we know it is this space in which God is moving moment by moment in a companioning session. It is so easy for that movement to be obscured by one or other of directee or director 'getting in the way' of what God might be about to do. Here is another important reason for every director to be in supervision – it is the place to take those times when we have noticed something has got in the way of a good enough companionship meeting.

A final word here about the concept of a 'holding

environment.' All change, learning and growth is painful and difficult (ask teenagers – they are doing it the fastest!). If there is to be transformation in the directee towards union with God this will be from time to time difficult and troublesome, often hard won through lots of tears. There is wisdom to be found from Donald Winnicott (1896–1971) and others who describe the creation of a safe enough 'holding environment' for change to take place. Key to this is the holding of boundaries around time, task and territory. Paying attention to beginning and ending a session, what we are there for (not counselling or problem-solving in ministry for instance) and the actual space of the room and who sits where are all vital to cultivating a fruitful environment for transformation. We will pick up these three boundary markers again in Chapter 3.

Much more could be said but perhaps the best approach here is to offer some other resources which encourage inter-disciplinary thinking in prayer and spiritual direction. The Ulanovs (*Primary Speech*) have written a definitive psychology of prayer and Philip Sheldrake's excellent *Befriending our Desires* takes up our theme earlier in the chapter of understanding the praying human being as one who is a desiring sexual person. There are good, if somewhat dated resources on Jung and the mid-life transition (Bryant, *Jung,* and Brennan and Brewi, *Mid-life Directions*). My friend and colleague Rosy Fairhurst has an excellent study guide to the question of *Uncovering Sin.*

Reflection and questions

- Have you noticed yourself reacting with heightened emotion to anything in this chapter? If so can you name that emotion and sense where it 'landed' in your body. What is that telling you?

- A human person is a being-in-communion where the self

is formed in relationship. How fruitful an idea is this for you and are there any further implications it might have in prayer, spirituality and companionship?

- What are your own views on the question of the brokenness of the image of God in humanity and how sin affects what happens in spiritual direction?

- How might you or those you direct be enabled to 'uncover' and work on sin?

- How important are the insights that a discipline like psychology can bring to spiritual direction? What would you like to know more about and how will you follow it up?

3

Jesus, God Incarnate; 'Turning Up'

In earlier chapters, we have affirmed that it is the nature of God to draw near to us out of the overflow of God's eternal loving relationships within Godself. People are made in the image of God as beings-in-communion. And yet all this has become broken and deeply fractured. Now we are ready to expand on that beginning because God draws near in order to rescue us, and indeed to rescue the whole cosmos.

Introduction

For Christians the rescue required by all of creation is effected by God drawing near to us *in Christ*. This chapter examines the implications for spiritual direction of God becoming human and the next chapter moves the discussion on as to how the rescue is achieved by Christ, particularly on the cross and in our salvation (and again what all this means for accompaniment). Overall, however, the nature of God's approach is not an intervention to do a job of work – 'the rescue' – but relational (being-in-communion again), to dwell with us 'in our flesh' (John 1.14) and, in the midst of our brokenness and sinfulness, start the process of rescue. This embodied presence, which we have grown used to Latinizing as 'the incarnation', is not the preamble to the saving work of Christ on the cross. It is the expression of God's intention, the acting out of that intention, and the means by which that intention – the rescue – becomes possible.

A recurring theme in these two chapters will be the so-called 'Christ-hymn' in Philippians 2.5–11. Here we have a fully rounded expression of what some refer to as the 'Paschal Mystery'. This idea is often kept to the events of the last week of Jesus' life which we celebrate from Palm Sunday to Easter Day each year. However, we believe it should properly refer to the whole movement from the annunciation to Mary as the God-bearer to the ascension of Jesus into heaven summarized so succinctly and beautifully in the Christ-hymn of Philippians. All of this matters, as it establishes the full humanity and divinity of the Christ, which we shall explore further in a moment. At this stage an important point needs to be made. The meaning of the 'Word became flesh' is that from the very beginning, at the annunciation to St Mary, humanity is incorporated in God. And Jesus Christ, as the Word made flesh, remains both fully God and fully human throughout his life, death and resurrection on the earth. Then, in exactly the same way, at the ascension Jesus takes humanity into the Godhead for all eternity. This is a permanent state of affairs. Humanity and God are inextricably joined in Jesus.

In our chapter at the start of this book looking at God we thought a lot about the Trinity and we'll spend more time studying the person and role of the Holy Spirit in another chapter soon. One of the implications of belief in the Holy Trinity is that we actually live our lives as Christians on the *inside* of God (Sherlock, 1991). Perhaps the prayer that captures this idea the best is that verse in St Patrick's Breastplate which describes Christ within and all about me. So we are clear that in spiritual direction it is God who directs, and the director is simply discerning, encouraging and accompanying that direction. I referred to the fire metaphor for spiritual accompaniment in the Introduction and it is worth returning to it here. As two people sit together attending to the movement of God they also do this *inside* God. That is, the warmth of the campfire presence of God in the room kindles further flames in directee and director. What we need to understand here is that the presence of God within the room and inside each participant in any spiritual direction session includes our own fullest humanity through what the Lord Jesus has accomplished for us. That humanity in no wise diminishes how Jesus is at the same time God. God is fully present in the room with us.

This is the hard-won doctrine of the incarnation, understood as a key part of the process of the rescue of the cosmos. Though it is inappropriate to use the language of 'rescue' with reference to the director/directee relationship, there is a creative synergy between what the incarnation accomplishes and the way in which we accompany others on their spiritual journey.

We're not going to spend a long time going into the detail of how the doctrine of the incarnation was forged (in the fires of biblical theology and Greek philosophy, at the very least) in the first centuries after Christ. However, when I first studied the subject many years ago, what I remember most is how the doctrine is largely framed in *negative* terms around how we should not think of who Christ is. This creates a kind of 'playing field' with specific boundaries which means there is leeway in how different people understand who Christ is and they remain Christians. Other views are held to be outside of the boundaries.

Thus Christ, in the classic definition, is affirmed as one single unified person with two natures – the fully human nature and the fully divine nature – and the four ways of understanding the one person and the two natures which are not permissible are

1. any mixing or 'hybridity' of the two natures – the identity of the two natures is in no way diminished by their unification in the one person;
2. any separation into two persons – there is not one human and one divine person;
3. any change, such that God becomes less than God as a human in Christ or that somehow the humanity of Christ is subsumed into divinity (God is just 'acting' at being a human); and

4. any division, such that the two natures exist alongside each other and are not unified in the one person.

Not many of us find it easy to access this kind of doctrinal statement. However, there might be some visual help in a famous sixth-century icon of Christ 'Pantocrator' (Ruler of All) which resides at St Catherine's Monastery next to the traditional Mt Sinai in Egypt. The icon writer attempts to depict the two natures in the face of the one person of Christ.[8] The two sides of Christ's face are painted differently and yet it remains one face to the viewer who is strangely attracted to this person. If either side is reproduced in mirror image the whole looks quite different. One side represents Christ as divine judge and the other as lover of humanity or 'good shepherd'. Whether this entirely works as a portrayal of the two natures in one person without 'mixing, separation, change or division' the reader will have to decide. It is certainly a brilliant attempt.

Understanding who Christ is and who Christ is not therefore has several implications for the task of spiritual direction. We note four, as a beginning here.

1 Incarnation, 'turning up' and empathy

God is prepared to assume our full humanity (Phil. 2.7) – not any lesser hybrid version of it or by pretending to be human in some way. God turns up among us and knocks around with us for 30 or so years (John 1.14 – my translation!) before announcing the Kingdom which 'has come near' (Mark 1.15) and beginning 'ministry'. Sam Wells has made this point forcefully in much of his recent writing, pointing out that *being*

---

[8] As an example of an explanation of the icon see https://orthodoxwiki.org/Pantocrator (accessed 11.4.2018) – many other examples and descriptions are available on a simple internet search. It is worth noting that the ancient Greek word for person is the same as the word for face.

with us takes up 90 per cent of Jesus' time on the earth (30 years) compared to the active 'ministry' time of three years (see *A Nazareth Manifesto*, 2015).

For some time now I have realized that about 80 per cent (perhaps even 90 per cent) of the effect of spiritual direction is found in simply turning up! The journey that someone has to make to sit in a room with an accompanier for an hour or so in order to attend to the activity of God in their life is often a long and difficult one and may even take years to accomplish for the first time. And this continues as long as the relationship goes on. Each time the energy and desire has to be found to arrive and settle into attending to what is often difficult and testing. There is a *kenosis* or self-emptying in coming to direction which is analogous to the self-emptying of Christ in Philippians 2.7. As a director, I know that there is usually something more pressing and urgent which will prevent directees from coming to the next session and it always tells me something when they forget the date, have to postpone or other things crowd out the possibility. However, the journey to a session can be important in itself. I noticed a difference in some of my directees recently when I moved about an hour further away from some of them. The time taken on the journey they now make to direction and the thoughts they have about what to discuss mean they seem more ready to get down to real work – not that what they prepare always becomes the subject of the session, sometimes God has other ideas.

On the other side of the equation directors (and counsellors) have long been used to the importance of empathy, though not always agreed on its exact meaning. For our purposes, it can be described as a key skill which enables us to value another, to listen to their story and to share in their feelings. This is sometimes called *somatic empathy* in that we feel the feelings of the other in our bodies. It is more than just being able to imagine ourselves into their situation; it is responsive and fully involved, without projecting on to the other person our own life experiences and emotions. It is costly, unlike just sympathy, and it does not leave us unchanged. What is important is that directors learn the skill of noticing where the feelings a directee evokes land in their body, take note of them and work with them, all the while staying in touch empathetically with the directee. This is about being simultaneously present to ourselves and to the other, which takes a lot of practice and reflection.

Though we are not used to describing God's approach in Christ through this category of empathy, it fits almost perfectly. Christ emptied himself in order to become for our sake as servant or slave, shared the lives of those who were willing to open themselves to him, never imposed himself on others, and all of this led him inexorably to the cross. When we share in the spiritual journey of another, we imitate Christ and his costly incarnation. This does not mean that we stand in the place of Christ, but it is one of the key ways in which the incarnation remains a present reality in the lives of those with whom we work.

2 Incarnation and identification

We can now move beyond empathy and discuss the implications of Christ being 'Emmanuel', God with us in both full divinity and humanity. The fourth-century bishop Gregory of Nazianzus (329–74) famously said that 'that which Christ has not assumed he has not healed' (Epistle 101). He was arguing in the particular and virulent theological debate of his age, as we have discovered, that Christ must be both fully human and fully divine. Taken more generally, this makes the point that divine empathy (God cared enough to come) is wonderful, but incomplete. The further wonder is that God in Christ took on our fractured humanity in his own person: 'Since, therefore, the children share flesh and blood, he himself likewise shared the same things ... and he had to become like his brothers and sisters in every respect' (Heb. 2.14, 17).

It follows that when we share someone's spiritual experience or life's struggle, we do so not from the outside, as detached professionals, but from the inside (and remember we are on the inside of God). We also share in their experiences and struggles. In a world of rapidly increasing professionalization and safeguarding, important though that is, we are called to a fuller and often riskier immersion, to a self-giving vulnerability – a *kenosis* on the part of the director which somehow meets that of the directee in their 'turning up'. We hurt not just for them, not just with them, but in our own personal places of pain as they share their brokenness with us.

This may at times lead us to an uncomfortable 'taking sides'. The point of the 'bias towards the poor' which liberation theology finds in the gospel is not that we give 'the poor' some kind of divine head start in the game of life. It is that our bias towards the poor draws us into an identification with them that may lead us to fight their battles with them (and suffer with them in the process). This too is an act of redemptive justice. In a more modest way, spiritual direction may involve us in the life battles of those who come for guidance. An incarnational approach which takes identification seriously may, on rare occasions, spill out of the direction session into a much less well-boundaried place.

All of this discussion of empathy and identification underlines the vital importance of supervision for all directors. If we are going to be 'incarnate' with the directee in the ways we have described, we should expect strong feelings to be raised in ourselves and the need for our own discernment on how much to identify with them and hold a strict boundary around a particular relationship or otherwise. We cannot do this alone, just as Christ as fully God had open channels of communication with the Father and the Spirit. Christ acted as one person and that person was being-in-communion (where the communion was unbroken or 'perfect'). So we too need a community of practice which enables us to create a safe enough space for us and the directee to be as close to our true selves as possible when we meet. In the same way as getting into the room is a challenge for the directee so getting into supervision by 'turning up' is the challenge for the director.

3 Incarnation and embodiment

Much of the material in the New Testament Epistles is dedicated to facing down that most insidious of all heresies, the Gnostic assumption that matter is in its very nature unclean and impermanent (like an early version of the modern sacred/secular divide). So there is a particular horror that God (conceived of as pure 'spirit') could get down and dirty with humanity. Salvation, in this scheme, involves rising above matter, discarding the body, either by totally denying it or by over-indulging it. We know that the form of Christianity the seventh-century prophet Muhammad was most likely exposed to was a Docetic form. Docetism has no problem with the resurrection of Christ, but is deeply offended by the idea that physical suffering might in some way be central to our salvation: 'They slew him not, nor crucified him, but he was made to *appear* to them like one crucified' (Al-Nisa', Chapter 4.158). The Docetists therefore denied that Christ was fully human because he was just appearing or pretending to be human.

This tendency to think of Jesus in a spiritualized way which denies the reality of the human body has long informed parts of the Church, and was further reinforced by a horror of sexuality and its accompanying 'pollution'. Spiritual direction that focuses on a life of contemplation and prayer to the exclusion of the embodied stuff of life perpetuates the heresy. Both the authors of this book, as noted earlier in the chapter on anthropology, say to potential directees that no area of life is automatically excluded from the conversation, and that one's physicality, including sexuality, is a potential area for exploration.

For those who accomplish some of their theological reflection through the creative arts (which in themselves re-enact the idea of embodiment), it is instructive to observe how representations of Jesus in his passion oscillate between stylized, almost ironed, out suffering which presents his body as clean, neat and glorious, and raw physicality that exposes the human horror. It is very hard to find works that capture the middle ground: enfleshed divinity.

Before we complete this section it is worth saying some more about why spiritual direction happens in the first place. Why do we need a spiritual director at all? In Protestant and Reformed theology it has been the received wisdom that there is only one mediator between us and God and that is the God-man Jesus Christ. This is fine while we are praying alone. The question is how do we find direction in that prayer? Can we do it alone? Just as humanity cannot save itself without the intervention of the Word made flesh, it seems, drawing on the long tradition of the whole Church, that we need to sit with another body if we are to inhabit prayer in ever deeper ways. This, as we have emphasized, does not make the director God, but at the very least makes God present in a different way than when we are alone.

In the spiritual direction room, God as being-in-communion with full humanity in Jesus is present in the space between the two participants. The two natures of Christ are available to the directee through the director tending to the campfire of God's presence. Here in the two natures is the possibility of 'love on the cold stone slab' as Thornton coined it – the human Jesus who loves as the good shepherd and the divine Jesus who is judge of all (Phil. 2.11), according to the Christ Pantocrator icon. Spiritual direction is an embodied spiritual practice which works because God became incarnate.

4 Living the incarnation – in the human and divine

We can take the truth of the two natures of Jesus further in setting the agenda for spiritual direction. Perhaps one of the questions we need to ask in direction is: how might we, following Jesus, become more human and more divine?

Jesus as portrayed in the Gospels lives closely with creation. For instance, I love Stanley Spencer's imagined extension of Mark 1.13, Jesus being with the 'wild beasts' during his temptations in the desert. Spencer paints Jesus carefully and lovingly holding a scorpion in his hands. Jesus comes to 'rescue' the whole of creation in some mysterious way which we do not yet see fulfilled (Rom. 8.22). Jesus' human embodiment is in creation and we, in our following of Jesus, cannot but be the same. Salvation has ecological implications, as the fifth Anglican mark of mission[9] reminds us: we are called 'to strive to safeguard the integrity of creation, and sustain and renew the life of the earth' because this is also what God does. We are rescued within the cosmic context, not despite it, as Paul says in Romans 11.15: 'For if their (the people of Israel's) rejection is the reconciliation of the world, what will their acceptance be but life from the dead!' 'World' here is the Greek *kosmos* – the whole universe.

How we treat our bodies and the creation around us properly features then in any rule of life a director may encourage in a directee. I sometimes wonder how much we can ask people about, for instance, how close they want to be to their recommended Body Mass Index or what percentage of their household waste is recycled. Are such questions too intrusive or simply part of what it is to be a faithful, embodied, 'earthy' Christian?

We have already mentioned Gregory of Nazianzus and he was also the first theologian to use the word *theosis* in relation to the divinization of the human person through baptism, which

---

9 The Five Marks of Mission were formulated by the Anglican Consultative Council in 1984, but are widely used in ecumenical contexts.

imparts the Holy Spirit and restores the true *image of God* in the believer.[10] Gregory works with the idea of the wonderful exchange; God becomes human in Christ so that we humans might become gods in our turn. This language sounds very strange to our ears but the idea of *theosis* is making a return in contemporary theology not least because of the upsurge of interest in spirituality. Gregory does not believe that in becoming divine we become somehow equal with God, but he does assert quite strikingly that through our baptism and the restoration of God's original image in us we can both act as God acts and be as God is. Even as I write it this way of thinking sends a shiver down my neck as it properly raises the stakes for directee and director alike. What else would the aim of accompaniment as *union* with God look like? Spiritual direction isn't, for example, some box-ticking exercise for a high-up who says we have to be in it to minister in their organization. No, it's rather like the famous story from the Desert Fathers[11] which goes like this:

> Lot went to Joseph and said, 'Abba, as far as I can, I keep a moderate rule, with a little fasting, and prayer, and meditation, and quiet: and as far as I can I try to cleanse my heart of evil thoughts. What else should I do?' Then the hermit stood up and spread out his hands to heaven, and his fingers shone like ten flames of fire, and he said, 'If you will you can become all flame.' (Ward, tr., 2003, p. 131)

---

10 I am indebted here in this paragraph to my friend, the theologian Gabby Thomas who wrote her PhD thesis in this area. See Gabrielle Thomas, *Divine yet Vulnerable: Gregory Nazianzen's Human Eikon*, Unpublished Ph.D Thesis (University of Nottingham, 2016).

11 There were some Desert Mothers too and they moved into the Egyptian desert from the fourth century onwards, as Christianity was adopted by the Roman Empire, in order to imitate Jesus facing his temptations and obey the instruction to 'pray without ceasing' (1 Thess. 5.17).

The Paschal Mystery and transformation

We summarize and conclude this chapter by returning to the Christ-hymn of Philippians 2. How are we transformed through prayer and spiritual accompaniment? How are we changed 'from glory into glory' – how do we become divine both in the act of baptism and in that baptism lived out in every moment of our discipleship every day?

Here we turn to some wisdom drawn from cultural anthropology which I have found enormously rich and fruitful over many years – and we'll need to return to it in the next chapter too.

More than a century ago an early anthropologist was studying the 'rites of passage' in an African tribe, particularly the age-mate rite of passage of adolescent boys from childhood to manhood. Over the space of a few weeks their social status (their 'being' if you like) is changed from boys to men. The anthropologist who discovered it says it happens like this. An age-mate group between perhaps 13–15 years old is identified by the village elders and they are 'stolen' out of their beds in the middle of night and taken to a secret, awesome place far away in the bush that only the elders know about. They experience this movement as chaotic and even traumatic but they must endure it. There they are taught about how to be men for several weeks by the elders and then at the end of that time the ritual ceremony (often involving some form of cutting the flesh) takes place, after which they return triumphantly to the village and everyone recognizes their new status in a big celebration. In the process this group of age-mates are 'bonded' for life; whatever their family status was back in the village this is equalized in the manhood camp. The whole is held and presided over by the elders who also preserve the 'holiness' of the place in the bush where the change takes place.

Anthropologists throughout the twentieth century theorized

about what was happening in such a transformation of being or status. They noticed the particularity of the place in the bush which was preserved for this one task – they called it the 'liminal' place after the Latin word *limen* meaning threshold; it is the edge or the gateway to the new way of being. The relationships among the age-mate boys that are equalized are characterized by *communitas,* where the normal social structures break down and a deep human bonding occurs. There is the separation phase that prepares for the new status and the re-aggregation phase that introduces them back into society with their changed status.

I have related all this because you might notice a connection between African rites of passage and the movement of Christ from heaven to earth and back again in the Paschal Mystery as we have understood it. In overall shape we call this a 'U' movement and there are specific tasks to attend to in each of the three phases; moving down the 'U' in separation, existing in the liminal, chaotic and often dark place at the bottom of the 'U' and then rising up to re-connect with life again by moving up the right-hand side. We'll address the bottom of the 'U' mainly in the next chapter but here we can think about the down and up legs. But first let's also make the connection with spiritual direction.

We can understand the place of spiritual direction as a 'liminal' space of transformation presided over by the director. Like the African elders they create it and 'hold' it for the directee, making it good enough and safe enough for them to go through the experience, just as Jesus is held by the Father and the Spirit throughout his earthly liminal journey. We have noted earlier how Jesus experiences *kenosis*, a *letting go* of equality with God in order to be born as one of us. We have seen how tough it is for some directees to get into direction in the first place and we now know more about why this might be. As we shall we see, the task at the bottom of the 'U' is *letting be* and as we emerge it is as if the future comes towards us (the proper realized eschatology in the now and not yet of the coming Kingdom inaugurated by Jesus) and so the task is *letting come*.

This movement mirrors my experience of the beginnings and endings of most direction sessions. The start is like a descent. Stories are told often on the surface of life and ministry and the temptation is to stay superficial and shallow and try and 'fix' presenting problems. The skilled director looks for the movements of consolation and desolation towards God in the stories and progressively peels back their layers or gets under the surface of them.

Towards the end of the session, and this can happen very rapidly, we let the intentions of the directee arise in them such that they can leave knowing there is newness coming which they are going to meet as they return, changed, to life back at home. In fact the whole notion of time in direction is a fascinating one since liminal space also seems to create liminal time where there is 'all the time in the world' for what needs to happen to happen. I relate this to the presence of God in Christ by the Spirit in the room and being inside the *eternal* God who has, literally, all the time in the world. I usually explain this phenomenon in relation to elite sports. Really brilliant sports people seem to have all the time in the world to do what they do, though of course they have trained extremely hard with their innate skills over many, many years. This is why watching elite sports is so attractive and beautiful for most people. My favourite example (being a bloke) is from football but you could find your own. I took my sons to a Cup Final in their teenage years and we sat very close to where, at a crucial point in the game, the ball dropped nicely for the hero of their team. It bounced up in front of him about twenty-five yards out from goal. As he shaped to shoot, time stood still and in that moment we all knew what was going to happen, as he did it – yes, he hit it into the top corner of the goaaaaal! We watched the future arrive in that split second and we never forgot the beauty of it.[12]

---

12 These ideas are related to the psychological concept of 'flow' popularized

This brings us to a final point from understanding direction as a liminal movement in fine tune with the whole Paschal Mystery. There has to be proper and effective *holding* that creates a safe enough or good enough space for the directee to explore the depths of the 'U'. This is one of the main tasks of the director in co-operation with God. We have already touched on boundaries in this chapter (as well as in the Introduction) and we turn again to them here because the way to create a safe enough space is for the director to stand at the boundary and decide what is let in or out and what is not. As we noted earlier, three main things need to be attended to at the boundary for the creation of safe space; they are: time, task and territory.

People feel safe when there is a clear, often ritualized beginning and ending and the amount of time given over to a 'normal' or regular session is agreed beforehand. I have a practice of beginning with silence and allowing the directee the first words when they are ready to speak. Endings vary but they are marked in deliberate ways. I think an hour plus or minus 10 minutes is normally ample for God to be at work.

Sticking to task will also help the directee to peel back the layers of their experience to reveal what God is up to. Being distracted by surface material as we have seen or straying into counselling for instance is not staying on task.

The territory is vital and needs to be maintained as a space dedicated to direction in my view. I remember once visiting a potential new director. The phone went twice in his office and he excused himself both times and answered it – I didn't go back. On the other hand, I was directing once in a particular place and something happened with a cat which we both saw through the window and it had a direct connection to what we had just been talking about. I allowed that in as it was clearly sent by God.

---

by Mihaly Csikszentmihalyi, see for instance his *Finding Flow: The Psychology of Engagement with Everyday Life*.

Reflection and questions

- Spend some time, even a few days, with Philippians 2.5–11. What do you notice most of all? Where do you currently identify yourself in the passage? How does the movement Christ makes relate to your own life experience?

- How difficult or easy is it for you to arrive at spiritual direction and perhaps supervision each time? What motivates you to make the journey? What obstacles do you habitually have to overcome?

- How helpful for you is the Christ Pantocrator image of the two natures of Christ in the one person? Which nature of Christ do you tend to be drawn to over the other – the human or the divine? Or perhaps this changes over time, so where are you at the moment? What difference does this make to you, to prayer, how you are directed or how you direct others?

- How do you react to the idea of *theosis* – the divinization of humanity? Firstly for you and then for any directees you might have? What difference might thinking about prayer and discipleship in these terms make?

- Do you recognize the stages of the 'U' movement in your experience of prayer and spiritual direction? How might you allow yourself to sink deeper into the experience of *letting go, letting be* and *letting come*?

4

Salvation and Transformation: Towards Union

Here we continue the theme of God coming near to us in Christ as rescue for humanity. What salvation is and how Christ achieves it on our behalf is our subject. These themes have profound implications for those offering and receiving spiritual accompaniment and so we reflect on the practical changes brought about in our lives by the actions of God.

Introduction

I have a vivid recollection from the early years of my ministry of meeting a young parishioner in a hospital chapel. She was recovering from drug misuse, and I was about to celebrate the Eucharist. In the few minutes that we had, she told me a little of her life's story and her experience of the highs and lows of cocaine use. We moved to the account of her dramatic and intense conversion to Christ, and she said that her first 'experience' of meeting the risen Christ was, 'the best rush I have ever had!'

In her case, the intensity of the experience and the rich feelings associated with it set her free from the need to seek drug-induced ecstasy ever again. There is of course a danger that in telling this story at the beginning of the chapter we seem to suggest that salvation is primarily experiential. The truth is rather that salvation is God's action on and in our lives. We experience this in the depth of our being, certainly, but it is not dependent on our experience for its efficacy. Salvation is first of all a free and unsolicited gracious act of God towards humankind: it is sheer gift. Then, and secondly, it is also a response to that act of grace in our own lives, which continues the process of rescue and restoration.

The other problem with my story is that it portrays salvation as a momentary act, a crisis or turning point, a threshold crossed. Some Christians talk as if that were the case. My father, who liked to mock this approach, told the story of a bishop who was approached by a zealous evangelist on a train.

'Bishop, are you saved?' he asked directly.

'Well, my man,' the Bishop replied, 'it all depends on whether you mean "have been saved", "am being saved" or "will be saved"!'

And of course, the story would have us understand that salvation is all three of those things, a past gracious act of God, a continuous and ongoing action in our lives, and the trusting hope that one day all will be well and we will be entirely safe.

What do we need saving from?

The title of this section makes a key assumption: that humans are in need of being saved, and Chapter 2 introduced the issue of sin, disordered desire and the dark side of life. Despite the fact that the concept of 'sin' is regarded as outmoded in our contemporary world, believers and non-believers alike know that human beings are frail and fractured in their creatureliness, incomplete in so many ways. Though we are often victims of the selfish and thoughtless actions of others, we know that we ourselves are also part of the problem. One of the great liturgical texts of the seventeenth century, the 1662 Book of Common Prayer, highlights both the internal and external aspects of our brokenness in the baptismal service, referring to: 'The devil and all his works, the vain pomp and glory of the world, with all covetous desires of the same, and the carnal desires of the flesh.'

SALVATION AND TRANSFORMATION: TOWARDS UNION

The inner/outer dynamic of our brokenness as troubled troublemakers is compounded by another dynamic, that of the individual and the community. Sin and evil are instigated by individuals and impact on individuals. However, because of the interconnectedness of all humanity and the social, economic and political structures that enable our mutuality, sin and evil are equally instigated by groups and impact on groups. In the past, sin has been excessively individualized, and the Church's insistence on personal sacramental confession led Christian society to think of each individual as sin-bearer. In this, we lost sight of the fault and deep structural sin of institutions, as the fourth Anglican mark of mission shows us: 'To transform unjust structures of society, to challenge violence of every kind and pursue peace and reconciliation.'

The Scriptures are clear about both of these dynamics: the inner/outer and the individual/corporate. It is also clear in scripture that the primary understanding of sin concerns creaturely disobedience towards God, who creates and sustains humanity. So we need saving from ourselves, and from those acts of cruelty and injustice perpetrated against us. But most of all, we need saving from an inappropriate prideful attitude towards God. The seventeenth-century poet John Milton tells us that it was pride that cast Satan out of heaven, and that with the help of his 'host of rebel angels' he aspired to 'set himself in glory above his peers' and 'to have equalled the Most High' (1990, p. 150). Milton's overworked demonology – from which some parts of the Church still suffer today – distracts us from the fact that we share in Satan's aspiration to equal the Most High God. Human pride is the worst poison of all.

The language of judgement and punishment, with which scripture is replete, is a response to human usurpation of the place of God. It may take the form of expulsion from Paradise, exclusion from the family, dislocation into exile, or a forensic declaration of guilt by the judge. Whatever metaphors are used, they express the fundamental dis-order that occurs when humans put themselves in the place of God, and they need to be read in this light. However, the language of guilt, blame and judgement can distract from the key message of scripture that God desires to rescue. There is a difficult balancing act here. If we privilege judgement, then we create a parodic theology of a vindictive god who is out to get us all. If we privilege rescue, we collude with a contemporary desire to create a god who is deep-down nice, and doesn't really mind what we do.

Both of these extremes surface in the conversation of spiritual direction and call for a particular theological alertness. On the one hand, those directees who tend to construct a judgemental 'god' out of their own mechanisms of self-blame need to be supported in their discovery of the radical meaning of grace. On the other hand, the 'gods of this present age' culturally predispose many to hedonistic theologies, in which the villains are those who spoil our pursuit of gratification and indulgence. Whether self-gratification or self-vilification is more likely to surface probably depends on the church culture that Christian disciples inhabit, and one should not presume that one or the other dominates.

The solution to this conundrum – and the answer to the two extremes – lies in the fact that God cares enough about us to want 'all manner of things to be well', in the words of Julian of Norwich. If God wished simply for revenge, then the story would have ended with that metaphorical all-drowning flood in Genesis 7. But God doesn't, and judgement becomes a step on the way to recovery and restoration. It would be too simple to say that redemption trumps judgement, but it is correct to state that God desires the restoration of a right relationship with humanity, and with me. Salvation is not a 'Get out of judgement free' card in a cosmic Monopoly game. Rather, God has come to the rescue, and goes on rescuing still.

SALVATION AND TRANSFORMATION: TOWARDS UNION

What happened on the cross?

The Prologues to the Fourth Gospel and to the Epistle to the Hebrews both make it abundantly clear that the rescuing intention of God reaches back to a time before time existed. John presents us with a Word which speaks light and life into the world from the beginning, a Word which according to Hebrews 'is the reflection of God's glory and the exact imprint of God's very being' (Heb. 1.3). In coming into this world, as the incarnate Jesus Christ, this 'Word made flesh' continues the work of rescue, as we have seen in the previous chapter.

And yet the incarnation also sets the stage for a journey of rescue which climaxes on and in the death of Jesus. William Tyndale, in his early sixteenth-century translation of 2 Corinthians 5.18, writes that: 'God … hath given unto us the office to preach the atonement.' It is one of the earliest technical uses of 'atonement', and the first time that a writer applies it to the rescuing work of God in Christ. The Greek word used by Paul means exchange or reconciliation, and most translators before and since Tyndale have used the language of reconciliation rather than this new-fangled sixteenth-century term.

It was at this point in the history of our language that the word became a technical one, so that we now often refer to the doctrine of the atonement as a kind of catch-all phrase for God's repairing of the divine relationship with humanity. There is no exact equivalent in any other language, a helpful reminder that talking about God is limited by our linguistic structures and vocabulary, and a caution against overloading any one word with exact meanings. That certainly is a salutary reminder for those of us who listen to the language used by those who come to us for guidance!

What Tyndale's word does make clear is that this work of divine recovery and reconciliation hinges most especially, uniquely, on the death and resurrection of Jesus Christ. To put it crudely, the doctrine of the atonement attempts to explain the 'mechanics' of what happened when Jesus died, and it is to this that we now turn.

The free gift of God

I said in the chapter introduction that 'salvation is first of all a free and unsolicited gracious act of God towards humankind'. Over the centuries, building on one group of images and metaphors in the biblical material, Christian theology has majored on human guilt and a forensic response, or human helplessness and divine gift, or human pollution and images of cleansing. All share a common emphasis that we cannot sort ourselves out. We are not deserving, we are not resourced, we are broken and cannot fix ourselves. In the spiritual life, this not infrequently leads to a sense of unremitting struggle, of failure or at times of deep despair.

Into this darkness Christ comes as the unsolicited gift of God's presence, underlining the seriousness of the human predicament and the radical and chaotic nature of human evil. God is not detached from the chaos, not disinterested and certainly not afraid to be sullied by it. In the categories of Chapter 3, God turns up and identifies with us, fully embodied in the person of Jesus Christ.

In the nineteenth century, with the growth of Enlightenment ideals and the 'civilizing' agenda of the industrialized nations, a natural evolution of humankind from worse to better, from morally inferior to superior was often taken for granted. Thankfully but tragically, the two major conflicts of the twentieth century disabused most of that thesis: the human propensity for evils of the most abhorrent kind has returned to haunt us. In a post-Christian age, however, the prevailing response is hopelessness, a sense of the meaninglessness of life and a fixation on making the most of life now.

Strangely, at this point post-Christian despair and the Christian gospel share a common perspective. Much of life is dreadful and suffering sometimes makes us wonder whether life is worth living. We are particularly convinced that 'sin matters' and that the world is broken, facing a crisis of apocalyptic proportions. At this point, the only way forward for post-Christian despair is avoidance and rage, whereas in Christian theology our attention is drawn away from ourselves and towards a God who enters the place of darkness with us.

In the context of spiritual direction, this underlies a truth that directors often miss. Because the doctrine of the atonement recognizes the depth of human evil as well as the wider political, social and ecological aspects of it, we are able to listen to the worst and darkest truths without being broken. We do not want to trivialize the heaviness of accompanying those who suffer or struggle, but here is a doctrine which is able to look deep into the darkness – the 'rough beast' of Yeats' poem 'The Second Coming' – without being overwhelmed.

From the perspective of the one being accompanied in direction, the underlying truth is that the inner darkness is not a place to be feared, but an approach to a spiritual threshold, a liminal place whose crossing enables the beginning 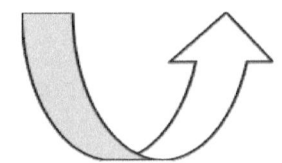 of change and personal transformation. To connect with the 'U' movement of the last chapter, on the cross Christ himself entered the place of desolation ('My God, my God, why have you forsaken me?' Matt. 27.46), pioneered this spiritual plumbing of the depths, broke the stranglehold of its fear and opened it up as a possibility for us all. In the language of 2 Corinthians 8.9: 'For you know the generous act of our Lord Jesus Christ, that though he was rich, yet for your sakes he became poor, so that by his poverty you might become rich.'

Over the years, in my preaching, I have drawn in the air over the pulpit the 'U' above to illustrate this passage of scripture, describing Christ's atoning journey which Paul then invites us to share in later in the same chapter. For Christian disciples, the descent is often the most feared. The worst desolating point is just before the very bottom – we do not wish to go further, we want to bale out. 'Going down the U' threatens to overwhelm us, to swallow us up. It echoes Jonah's psalm of lament from the belly of the great fish: 'You cast me into the deep, into the heart of the seas, and the flood surrounded me; all your waves and your billows passed over me' (Jonah 2.3). The gift that Jesus gives us in his passion, dereliction and death is the insight that entering the darkness opens the possibility of change, of salvation. What seems to be the end of me may be only the beginning of a new life.

This is not to trivialize or diminish the pain and desolation. It is simply to demonstrate that Christ's pioneering descent into hell

1. broke the chains of darkness (1 Peter 3.18–20);
2. showed us that in the deepest darkness, he accompanies us; and
3. leads towards an ascent into a place of light, the 'inside' God, as we noted in Chapter 3.

One of the great Christian poems of the nineteenth century, Francis Thompson's 'Hound of Heaven', illustrates graphically the torment of the opium addict descending to the hell of self-destruction as a fugitive from God, yet experiencing in that very descent Christ's presence as a pursuing hound, release, and hope of freedom. The poem draws to a close with the words of Christ: 'Rise, clasp my hand, and come!'

Close to the bottom of the 'U' is the threshold, the place of darkness and of desolation.[13] There is a secular though spiritually charged equivalent to this in the book *Presence: Exploring Profound Change in People, Organizations and Society*, which speaks of the Theory 'U' as a new mode of learning where at the bottom of the U, on the threshold, we 'presence' ourselves, 'seeing from the deepest source and becoming a vehicle for that source' (Senge et al, 2005, p. 89). There we become totally and utterly dependent on the ground of all being, which we call God. From our Christian perspective, we can say that the greatest gift of God in Christ's desolation is God's being present with us, his opening of the door, his traverse of the threshold with us into a world replete with new possibilities, yet to be realized.

The prodigal gift

Many of us are familiar with the niceties of social courtesy. We ask ourselves what kind of gift is appropriate to take when we are going to a dinner party, or simply visiting a new neighbour. This isn't necessarily grudging, but demands a fine balance of good manners, kindness and the avoidance of embarrassment. The story of God's gift is quite remarkably different: it is a gift of presence, which is not limited, boundaried or conditional. It is prodigal because it is given without measure and without being tailored to the expected response. Spiritually – and this is one of the wonderful 'tools' in the director's kit – it brings deep assurance when this truth about the divine hospitality is accepted.

When the Wesleys returned from the American colonies to England in 1737 with their tails between their legs, their 'holiness project' in tatters, the one ray of light on their horizon was a memory from two years earlier, as they had sailed out.

---

13 Though it is tempting to equate this with St John of the Cross's description of the 'dark night of the soul', that phrase does not encompass all liminal experiences of disorientation, desolation or dislocation.

Then, John Wesley, terrified of the sea, wrote in his diary of the storm in which 'a terrible screaming began among the English. The Germans calmly sung on. I asked one of them afterward, "Were you not afraid?" He answered, "I thank God, no" (6 February 1736).

The subsequent experience of a heart strangely warmed at the Fetter Lane Moravian Chapel in Aldersgate is often described as a conversion. This puts the emphasis on what happened to the Wesley brothers. More important by far than the experience is the underlying truth that God approaches humans in their moments of greatest helplessness and gives them what they cannot themselves obtain or attain to. In the words of Romans 5.6: 'While we were still weak, at the right time Christ died for the ungodly.' This gift of ungrudging grace is given to the most undeserving. The good news that we have for those we direct is that God has already put in place everything that we need for full rescue and complete restoration. The past tense of 'save' is 'already saved'.

In the current climate of institutional decline in the Church, the pressure to perform seems inexorable. Whether this pressure is self-imposed or laid on us externally, the relief of not having to work at earning God's approval is critical to healthy ministry in all God's people. It is important to understand that this is not a simplistic faith/works issue, nor a debate about whether we are to be actively involved in our own salvation. It is simply the bedrock of the doctrine of atonement that God acted first, decisively, irreversibly, for humankind and not against us. The best spiritual direction leads people away from a performance-driven life to an assured relational life with God. Only then can we begin to talk about faithful response.

The nature of God's action

Having established *that* God acts to save us, and acts unstintingly,

SALVATION AND TRANSFORMATION: TOWARDS UNION

we need to think a little about how God accomplishes this, while recognizing that the various theories of atonement are (necessarily limited) motifs or metaphors rather than mechanisms. Historically, the prevailing motifs have been those of ransom, substitution and sacrifice. Each can be found in some form in the Christian Scriptures, each has something to teach us about God's action, and each has problematic elements.

'Ransom' is found on the lips of Jesus himself in the Gospels of Mark and Matthew, and along with the word 'redemption' hints at buying back that which is lost in captivity: the human person, or the human race. Its merit is that it suggests restored status (ownership, freedom from slavery or from kidnap). Those who are ransomed or redeemed are returned to their 'true family'. Of Jesus it is said in Revelation 5.9: 'By your blood you ransomed for God saints from every tribe and language and people and nation.' It is problematic in that it can seem as though God is in some way paying the devil to get us back, an entirely unbiblical image.

The idea of the substitution of an innocent victim to replace a guilty party is often underpinned by the language of Isaiah 53.6: 'The Lord has laid on him the iniquity of us all.' It underscores the seriousness of sin and the demands of justice, while reminding us that when something is damaged or destroyed, reparation is often expected. If I cannot rescue myself, another must stand in my place or pay for my misdemeanour. However, much as I am a fan of pre-Raphaelite art, even I find William Holman Hunt's representation of the scapegoat in Leviticus difficult to stomach. The animal is beautifully groomed, passive, just there, in the midst of a bleak and violent landscape, to be punished for the sins of Israel. No wonder some modern theologians speak of 'divine child abuse'.

These motifs can so easily be read to suggest that violence can only be offset by violence, sin by sacrifice, misdemeanour by penalty. Not a few sermons and recent hymns on the subject have suggested that an angry Father has to be pacified by a victim Son, completely fracturing the unity of the Holy Trinity. At the heart of Old Testament religious practice, of course, we find the principle of sacrifice, carried through into the Epistle to the Hebrews' account of the meaning of the death of Christ: 'He has appeared once for all at the end of the age to remove sin by the sacrifice of himself' (Heb. 9.26). And it is here that we can begin to make sense of the objective action of God. God does not uphold justice or holiness by exacting a penalty from another. God alone, human and divine, stands in our place and is poured out in love and self-offering for us. While Jürgen Moltmann's theological approach may not suit everyone, the title of his book *The Crucified God* makes the point perfectly. No one is crucified but God embodied in our human form. God bears the weight of our sin entirely, and in bearing that weight, is fully satisfied. We are fully ransomed!

There are two aspects of spiritual direction that emerge from this discussion around the gifted act of God's grace. We have already drawn attention to the first: that a healthy Christian journey is only possible when we are assured of the unconditional love of God. Yet in our experience, many Christians and Christian leaders doubt their acceptability before God. I once had a bizarre conversation with a depressed Christian who asked me if God was on her side. I should have known better, but I quoted Romans 8.1 to her: 'There is therefore now no condemnation for those who are in Christ Jesus.' She immediately came back at me with the riposte, 'But how can I know if I am in Christ Jesus?'

In her depression, uncertainty and anxiety were to be expected. Perhaps in the stresses and strains of ministry, the same uncertainty and anxiety will flourish. That of course is why our confidence needs to rest in a theological absolute rather than a shifting set of emotions. God is on your side.

The only way is up

When we and those to whom we minister have the courage to descend with Christ into the place of darkness, however we conceive it in our own journey, we arrive at the threshold where we may begin one of many crossings into new life. This is where the second part of the redemptive process unfolds, our response to God's gift in Christ. The classic language of spirituality for this redemptive process is summed up in the three stages of *purgation, illumination* and *union*. We will consider each of these in turn, bearing in mind that the process is not linear but spiral. We go round the three stages over and over again in the course of our life with God, and each time we move a little forward. So this is not a masterclass on how to become super-spiritual, merely a celebration of the possibility of 'upward' movement.

Purgation

The word 'purgation' conjures up unfortunate images to the modern mind. Perhaps the more accessible modern metaphor is that of deep cleaning, or cleansing. It is hard work, a necessary negative, which leads to sparkling change. First of all, it is experienced through the practice of silence, in which we acknowledge that we have nothing to bring or give to our relationship with the divine that will make things better. In silence we discover the hardest truth of all that no spiritual activity can persuade God to look on us with greater favour. In silence, we abandon our grandiose dreams of 'making ourselves better Christians'.

In the Western Church up to the sixteenth-century Reformations, purgation was more commonly associated with the Sacrament of Confession. Since the Reformation, Protestant Christians have been uncomfortable or antagonistic towards the idea, and have lost something valuable along the way. Christians from a Catholic tradition continue to value the sacramental work of purgation, now referring to the Sacrament of Penance and Reconciliation.

As someone who grew up in an Anglo-Catholic tradition, I was schooled to make my confession on a regular basis, starting with the Saturday before my confirmation at the age of nine. Sixty years later, I can still recall the enormous sense of relief and closure that accompanied the painful act of admitting my foolish and small sins to the confessor, his wise advice and especially the words: 'Go in peace. The Lord has taken away your sin, and pray for me, a sinner.'

While Anglican practical theology has wisely never insisted on forms of public, quasi-sacramental confession, it has suffered from a lack of confidence in inviting people to bring their besetting sins and addictions 'to the altar', along with the sense of shame, stain, failure and despair that many carry alone in their spirits. There is here an opportunity for a remarkable coming together of theology, psychology and spirituality, in which past traumas may be put to rest. At least, the process of healing is started.

Discerning when it is proper to offer a formal liturgical act of this nature is not simple, though the clues often lie in the subject's self-presentation. Those include a conviction that God needs to be addressed directly and contritely; a sense that the act or sin cannot be dismissed with a simple apology but requires a more serious, semi-public forum; or a desire to hear formally from God that the sorrow has been heard and accepted. As this is an uncommon practice in many Christian traditions today, even of a more Catholic type, directors may need to let clients know that it is available, and how it may be accessed. If a director comes from a tradition in which only the ordained may carry out this function, then she should know who might appropriately be approached with such a request.[14]

---

14 The Anglican 'Common Worship' book entitled 'Christian Initiation' is a

SALVATION AND TRANSFORMATION: TOWARDS UNION

Illumination

Deep cleaning is never an end in itself in the spiritual life. It clears the way for a more wholesome and fuller engagement with God, in which we are 'insided', included and incorporated into Christ. In the last chapter, reference was made to 'the warmth of the campfire presence of God'. Here we'll use the associated metaphor of illumination. Holding together these twin images is a helpful reminder of the fact that the divine light is not merely external to us. Certainly, light shines outside and beyond us, to guide and lead us. But it also, equally importantly in the Christian tradition, shines and burns within. In the language of the East Anglian 'Family of God' in the sixteenth century, we are 'godded with God.'

There are three facets to illumination, all of which inform this part of the spiritual life. They are example, teaching and indwelling light. The exemplary light of Christ is the means by which God shows us the way of union, the possibility of the way, and God's own accompaniment of us on the way. God will never run ahead of us to leave us behind. I've already drawn attention to the fact that the really dark places of life, the thresholds at the bottom of life's 'U' are the places where transformation becomes possible. As a result, there is an irony or paradox, that darkness is often the place where the clearest light becomes visible. The dark night of the soul lightens our way towards union with God. It is the light of that union.

So while the late medieval spiritual tradition in the West often focuses on positive light, as in Richard Rolle's *The Fire of Divine Love*, there is a parallel tradition in works like *The Cloud*

---

good place to look for advice in the 'Introductory Note to The Reconciliation of a Penitent'. Though readers from a different Christian tradition may find the formal language unfamiliar or awkward, it is important to understand that momentous occasions in life need the safety, containment and strength of such language.

of Unknowing, where it is only by embracing the darkness that we enter the divine light, and become 'godded with God'.

> Then perhaps he will at times send out a beam of spiritual light, piercing this cloud of unknowing that is between you and him, and show you some of his mysteries, of which human beings are not permitted or able to speak. Then you will sense your feelings aflame with the fire of his love. (*Cloud of Unknowing*, 2001, p. 52)

Strikingly, it is this tradition which informed the early sixteenth-century Spanish Catholic mystical tradition of *Los Alumbrados* (literally The Enlightened Ones) and was so formative of the spiritual thought of Teresa of Ávila and John of the Cross himself.

Spiritual directors are naturally suspicious in the present climate of suggesting that those they direct might follow their example thoughtlessly, fearing the development of a dependent relationship or one compromised by transference. However, we might as well bite the bullet and recognize that many come to us for direction because they trust us and – dare we hint at it – see something of the divine light in us. It is better to acknowledge this, accept its giftedness as a particular ministry, and learn how to work with it humbly and graciously. Exemplary relationships in spiritual direction are perhaps best understood as mutual: we act as examples to each other.

The second facet of illumination is what Clement of Alexandria in the early third century called 'the divine *gnosis*', or knowledge. 'Knowledge ... is the illumination we receive, which makes ignorance disappear, and endows us with clear vision' (Clement, *Paidagogus* 6). Building on the fierce debate hinted at in 1 Corinthians, where spiritual elitism had crept into the Church, Paul insists that we must be taught Christ, and teach Christ. This is 'insider' information, available to all, through no human cleverness, but only through knowing Christ in his incarnation, suffering, death and resurrection. Most importantly here, for the task of spiritual direction, is our understanding that we are not enlightened by a set of doctrinal formulae. We are enlightened by the light that has come into the world, Jesus Christ. Liz Hoare puts it well in *Using the Bible in Spiritual Direction*: 'In Christian spiritual direction there is an assumption that both [director and directee] will share the Jesus story and the Christian creeds' (2015, p. 10).

The third facet is that of 'indwelling light', towards which John the Evangelist points in the Prologue to the Gospel: 'The true light, which enlightens everyone, was coming into the world' (John 1.9). Recently I saw a dying tulip backlit by the sun, and was astonished by its translucence. As the sun shone through the wilting petals, they took on a new life of glory. It's this 'enlightening' that Paul refers to in 2 Corinthians 4.6, where he says that God: 'Has shone in our hearts to give the light of the knowledge of the glory of God in the face of Jesus Christ.' Both John and Paul give us the image of an external source of light that shines in from the outside, and inhabits or indwells us. To change the metaphor, the Holy Spirit imprints the character of God in us.

In Chapter 5 we will explore further what this means for the pursuit of holiness in the Christian life. For now, suffice to say that holiness is not a struggle to please God by achieving ever higher levels of good behaviour. It is the result of a growing and transformative intimacy with God. Though the spiritual director may often have cause to address issues of sin and holiness, the fruit of change comes from encounter, intimacy, and ultimately union with God.

Union

The Christian mystical tradition has not infrequently been accused of implying a kind of pantheism in which we are absorbed into the Godhead (we referred to these questions when discussing *theosis* in the last chapter). Such a breaking down of the difference between creator and creatures is alien to Christian theology, but it is also possible to overplay that difference. The redemptive process whereby we are drawn back to God, and into God, has as its final goal complete *union* (but not absorption) within the Holy Trinity. We retain our identity, our distinctiveness, our humanity, but no longer at the cost of separation from God.

The New Testament develops the theme of union most fully in the language of 'in Christ'. To be a Christian at all is to be 'in Christ Jesus' (Rom. 8.1). The whole of the redemptive journey, and its attendant gifts, happens 'in Christ Jesus' as well: 'God ... establishes us with you in Christ' (2 Cor. 1.21). Here, additionally, we are reminded that union with Christ is primarily corporate rather than individual. It becomes more dramatic and intimate in Galatians 2.20: 'It is no longer I who live, but it is Christ who lives in me.' The interpenetrative language of this verse is underplayed by those who fear the mystical tradition, but there is no doubt that Paul conceives of the Christian life as one in which we are drawn into the Godhead in (and not just through) Christ. Even more, the Godhead is described by Jesus as being drawn into us in the remarkable 'abiding' language of John 15. We could remind ourselves here of the story told in the last chapter of the two monks in the desert which ends in the assertion: 'If you will, you can become all flame.' Here, our union with God is like the burning bush (Ex. 3.1–6), in-flamed and touched to its core, but not consumed by the divine presence.

The fourteenth-century mystic Jan van Ruusbroec (1293–1381) describes this union with God as well as anyone in his *Spiritual Espousals*:

> Sometimes those who live the interior life turn in within themselves ... following their inclination to delight, and there

SALVATION AND TRANSFORMATION: TOWARDS UNION

… they look with a simple and inward gaze upon blissful love.

In so contemplating God:

They overcome God and become one spirit with him. And in this union in the spirit of God they savour an ecstatic delight, and possess the divine essence. (Davies, ed., 1989, p. 95)

In an over-sexualized age, commentators find it only too easy to imply that such language is erotic, and St Teresa's experience of an arrow piercing the soul is often read in the same way. In a less suspicious age readers will have apprehended the central message of this mystical experience as intimate union with God. Of course, one form of ecstasy is physical love. Here, the physical experience is a metaphor for fulfilment and a togetherness that no longer needs analysis. It just is what it is. I and God are one: in that I rest.

In an over-busy and driven world, mentors and coaches spend much of their time encouraging clients to centre themselves, practising mindfulness and centering their lives and their beings. If the idea of union with God in Christ means anything, then *spiritual* direction will focus on attentive mindfulness to the reality, presence and engagement of God. From there, it will accompany people towards a centre which is both beyond them and attainable by them: the unmediated presence of God. Rest, in that sense, is not about motionless contemplation but about circling around the divine centre and regularly 'coming in to land'. Union with God is about coming home.

Given that we are in transition in this life, union with God involves keeping on keeping on. Even for St Teresa, her ecstatic experience of the wounding arrow of love doesn't take away the need to care for her community. One of the most remarkable sermons of St Bernard of Clairvaux, one of the earliest leaders of the Cistercian order, expounds a verse in the Song of Songs as a series of kisses in which we progressively kiss the feet of Christ (in repentance), the hands of Christ (in service) and then the lips of Christ (in union). Extraordinarily, though, precisely at the point at which he begins to speak of union, he breaks off the sermon to enjoin the brothers to go and serve the visitor who is even then knocking at the door of the monastery. So too we who long for deeper union with Christ find ourselves daily drawn back into the world by the intimate love of God.

Herein lies the ongoing tension between our longing for God, and our longing for the world to know God. In this life union is fundamentally missional. We who experience the heart of God share God's weeping heart for this world. That tension is well expressed in 2 Peter 1.3–4, in which we learn that we are given

1. everything that we need for life (salvation);
2. everything that we need for godliness (holiness and transformation);
3. the opportunity to escape corruption (purgation);
4. the knowledge of him who called us by his own glory and goodness (illumination); and
5. participation in the divine nature (union).

Conclusion

In our pursuit of union with God, there is always the danger that we individualize the quest and isolate ourselves from other disciples. This will be addressed in Chapter 8's exploration of ecclesiology. For now, it is worth noting that the repeating upward journey of faith, through purgation and illumination towards union is formally and liturgically acted out in the great sacrament of baptism. So for Paul in Romans 6, in baptism we die to sin and rise to new life in Christ. Then in Romans 8, the great 'union' chapter, he reminds us that this new life is life 'in Christ' who dwells in us. Baptism serves as the formal performance – the effective sign – of all that Christ's redeeming work accomplishes for, with and within us. It may well be, then, that in working with a client who longs for closer union with God, we need to encourage not only spiritual commitment and persistent journey but the willing step of (irreversible) baptism as a key to the faith journey.

Reflection and questions

- How do we hold together 'judgement and rescue' and avoid a vindictive god as well as an all-permissive one? How does accompaniment help us here?

- Words traditionally attributed to St Richard of Chichester offer thanks to God for 'all the gifts which you have given me, and all the pains and insults you have borne (or carried) for me.' How might you describe the 'gifts' and 'pains' in the dynamic of your relationship with God? How are these dealt with well in companion relationships?

- Can you identify a spiritual threshold which has taken you into a place of darkness? If so, reflect on how you moved from fearing it to seeing it as a place of possibility. As a director or directee how might you be enabled to go to this place? What could hold you safely enough as you move through the bottom the 'U'?

- In the spiritual task of purgation, what are your needs, and how might you and God together engage in that process? What's the role of a good accompanier in this stage of the journey?

- The sacrament of baptism is the outward sign of the purgation, illumination and union with which God gifts us. Reflect on the ongoing outworking of your baptism, either by thinking through your active or inherited memory of it, or by re-reading key parts of the baptismal liturgy. What difference might this make to a companion or pilgrim?

5

The Holy Spirit and Companionship

Now we turn to think about the Holy Spirit as a person rather than an experience, who brings the beyond near through creativity, in our giftings, and in words and silence. The same Spirit wells up within us in prayer and in our journey of holiness, and drives us out to share in the mission of God. Spiritual companionship seeks to enhance all of these aspects of the work of the Spirit within us and without us.

It has often been said that after the sixteenth-century Reformations, the Protestants had for their Trinity the Father, the Son and the Holy Bible, whereas Catholics contented themselves with Father, Son and Holy Eucharist. Western Christianity has certainly struggled to make sense of the doctrine of the Holy Spirit, who is in the popular mind little more than the power of God, a divine force that pervades creation, our spirits, our communities and our churches.

I certainly hadn't thought much about the Holy Spirit in my growing years, and I recall little preaching on the matter beyond my father's regular retelling of the Pentecost story every Whitsunday. So when I arrived at university in England in 1968 in the middle of what came to be known as 'charismatic renewal', I was more than a little bemused. After about 18 months of heady debate between conservatives and charismatics, I found myself persuaded by Pentecostal arguments about 'the baptism in the Holy Spirit'. By 1971, to put it crudely, I wanted what Pentecostals claimed to have. One summer Sunday afternoon, with three charismatic monks from the Community of the Resurrection, my fiancée and two friends, we gathered to pray in the guest house chapel at Mirfield in West Yorkshire.

For some time, nothing happened. Then one of our number said, 'Get out of the boat', words that he later described as his 'first word of prophecy'. I don't know what I did, but – control freak that I am – I let go, and began to 'speak in tongues'. At first it was exhilarating, then exhausting and finally embarrassing, as I couldn't stop. I had to be led by the hand through the college corridors babbling away, hoping in the other part of my mind (the logical, organized part!) that I wouldn't bump into anyone.

That experience has journeyed with me over many years, and I have never lost the sense of being 'set free' by it. I've wrestled with it, not least with the particular language of charismatic Christianity. I've been nourished by it, and it has shaped my life of worship and prayer in many ways. It remains a key 'event' in my personal Christian calendar as well as an area of ongoing academic research.

Most importantly, what happened to me on that day is an 'it', an event, an experience. 'It' is *not* the Holy Spirit, and it is as tempting for some of us to turn the Holy Spirit into an experience as it has been for the popular mind to make the Holy Spirit a power of God. This is why sometimes we hear the Holy Spirit referred to as 'it' since it is the experience rather than the person the people are remembering. No experience of God is God, however much it may point towards God, and in direction we need to keep the distinction in focus.

Holy Spirit is personal

The doctrine of the Holy Trinity (see Chapter 1) traditionally describes the Holy Spirit as

- fully God;
- fully personal; and
- fully distinct from the Father and the Son as the third person of the Trinity.

THE HOLY SPIRIT AND COMPANIONSHIP

For us, in a less systematic thought-world, it suffices to say that we encounter Holy Spirit personally as God who comes to us from far beyond and from deep within. The result of that encounter may sometimes be powerful, a disconcerting or overwhelming experience, but we must be careful not to confuse the meeting with the One we meet. As we have noted, the meeting is an object, an 'it', but the One we meet is a person. We would do well to talk of 'Holy Spirit' at this point, rather than 'the Holy Spirit', which makes Holy Spirit sound like a substance (again)!

In Chapter 1 we spoke briefly about the transcendence and the immanence of God. The first thing that encounter with the Spirit of God does is to bring to us a profound sense of the 'beyondness' of God, the God who is other than us, greater than us, not containable or measurable by us, yet who chooses to approach us. This way of encounter is perfectly described by the German philosopher Rudolf Otto in his classic *The Idea of the Holy* as *mysterium tremendum et fascinans*, a mystery which is both terrifying and deeply attractive, the cliff edge to which we are drawn even as it churns our stomachs! Through the work of the Holy Spirit, the unfathomable mysteries and wonders of the cosmos are brought personally close, which belies some versions of the idea of transcendence as the unreachableness of God. Through the approach and work of the Holy Spirit, we are drawn into the beyondness of God.

The other half of this is that the God who comes to us from far beyond also comes to us from deep within. This is the 'immanence' of God, the 'inside-me' or 'inside-us' that is a key feature of the doctrine of the Holy Spirit. The word that best describes this is 'intimacy', from the Latin adverb *'intus'* or within. Here the best metaphor is that of the spring of water bubbling up from the inside out, to which the Gospel of John makes reference: 'As the scripture has said, "Out of the believer's heart shall flow rivers of living water"' (John 7.38). The doctrine of the Holy Spirit in the Christian tradition holds these two equal and opposite truths together in a powerful tension, and both truths inform the practice of spiritual direction quite profoundly. They will serve as the structure for the central part of this chapter, but first we must attend to the matter of gendered language for the Holy Spirit.

The Holy Spirit and gender

English speakers are habituated to the idea that anything personal is gendered, a 'he' or a 'she'. Attempts to remove such gender-specific language from the Bible and from Christian theology have been variably successful, and deeply controversial in some circles. Because the first two persons of the Trinity have historically been given masculine names, some commentators have argued for a feminine gendering of the Holy Spirit. Attention is drawn to the fact that '*ruach*' (Spirit or breath in Hebrew) is a feminine noun. Further, there is a strong link between the Holy Spirit and 'Wisdom', *Sophia* (also feminine) in Greek. The classic popular version of this is in William Young's parable-novel *The Shack*, where the Asian Sarayu is the Spirit-person (2007, p. 87).

There are some problems with this approach. Though in incarnate form the second person of the Trinity is a man, God is not inherently male in any of the three persons. The Word of God as pre-existent second person of the Trinity is linguistically masculine in Greek (*Logos*) but not essentially male. This is also true of the first person. Though one of the dominant biblical metaphors for this person is 'Father', it is counterbalanced by a plethora of feminine images (midwife, she-bear, mother hen, baker-woman, among others: Mollenkott, *The Divine Feminine*) to draw attention to the fact that 'Father' gives us not a masculine God but a creative, loving, hospitable and family-making God. Interestingly, Sarah Coakley in *God, Sexuality and the Self* says that the feminist '*must*' call God Father for: 'It lies with her alone to do the kneeling work that ultimately slays patriarchy at its root' (p. 327).

We who are created in the image and likeness of God (Gen. 1.27) are, as already made clear in Chapter 2, made individually women and men in community, each reflecting a part of a God who is not man, not woman, not both, not neither, but embracing in totality all aspects of all of us. To attribute specific gender to one or other person of the Holy Trinity is unhelpfully to turn parts of God into female or male role models.

The spiritual director will come across individuals in the course of her work for whom either male or female metaphors are unhelpful. The solution is not to turn God into someone whose gender is more congenial (a mother for the person who was abused by his father) or more reassuring (a father-figure for those who experienced deep abandonment). Rather, it is to help the one we accompany to come to terms with their own boundaried (or uncertain) gender identity in the light of a God who loves them for who they are uniquely, and offers them all that is good in our experiences of the human male and female psyches. Yet at the very least, we need to be aware of the gendered nature of the language we use, the traps that this language lays for us, the associations which it may have in the mind and life of a directee. We may also want to listen out for the particular language used by that person, and self-induced difficulties that may result.

Through the Spirit, the beyond is brought near: creativity

In Chapter 1 the nearness of God was portrayed as an act of approach and an act of hospitality. Now we further explore that nearness as a series of actions and gifts from the Holy Spirit.

The first, perhaps primary action of the Holy Spirit towards the world is the work of inspiration, in-breathing, where the breath breathed in remains part of the one into whom the breath is breathed. Intriguingly, 'to inspire' means both 'to breathe in' and 'to breathe into'. So the action of inspiration which is specially the work of the Spirit involves God breathing into us life and the gifts of life (God inspires us) and us breathing in deeply and receiving the gifts of life and creativity. We bring both senses together in saying that the Holy Spirit gives us access to the creativity or creative breath of God.

The Spirit inspires all human beings, of course, and in this inspiration Christians find the source of all artistic endeavour. This point is crucial to a proper understanding of how the Spirit works beyond and often despite the boundaries we place on God. The fact that I am a Christian in no sense makes me a better artist than the next person, though my faith in some sense will make me a different kind of artist. To be an artist is to share in the ongoing work of God's creation, whether we know it or not, whether we believe it or not.

The often-quoted model for this is the narrative of Oholiab and Bezalel in the book of Exodus who are inspired: 'by the Spirit of God, with spirit, intelligence and knowledge in every kind of craft' (Ex. 35.31). What can be missed in this formalized story of the building of the Tabernacle is the responsive stirring of the heart which is required: 'Everyone whose heart was stirred to come to do the work' (Ex. 36.2). The artistic endeavour is both a receiving of gifting and talent *and* the willingness to risk using it. This brings us on to a further sense of inspiration that is pertinent here. That is the call on the spiritual director to inspire (or encourage inspiration in) those they accompany, using his or her inspiration as director, in order to accompany that person into the freedom of full creative humanity. Living is a risky business in itself, and many of us protect ourselves against failure, shame, embarrassment or the criticism of others by living below our full potential, the 'abundant life' of John's

Gospel. The wisdom of the Holy Spirit given to the director invites the directee to step into the new place (the place of the threshold referred to already in Chapters 3 and 4) and try out new things.

The Welsh priest-poet R. S. Thomas put it this way in the poem 'Poetry for Supper' (1993, p. 86):

Listen, now, verse should be as natural
As the small tuber that feeds on muck
And grows slowly from obtuse soil
To the white flower of immortal beauty.

It is worth reading on further into the poem, which is itself an invitation into the artistic endeavour by risking the struggle of creativity. For now, it is sufficient to remind ourselves as directors that the Holy Spirit is asking us to call others into new journeys, adventures or pilgrimages, to learn again to play and experiment, to rediscover long-suppressed ways of being that came naturally to us once. Extending our discussion of creativity a little further, we also observe that the doctrine of the Holy Spirit demands of spiritual direction a radical refusal to separate life into artificial categories of 'natural' and 'supernatural', or to focus on certain features of the pilgrim's life as more 'spiritual' than others.

Conversation between director and directee may and will sometimes encompass earthy, fleshy, creative, sensual elements. In fact one of us, at least, is sure a companion has 'landed' with us when they are free to swear out loud. Directors may also wish to discuss with directees whether different models of direction might include movement or play. The traditional setting for direction tends to be the study or room set apart. Some of those I accompany find face to face conversation quite difficult, and for those, the side by side position of walking is less awkward, and invites greater honesty. Others find it difficult to sit still, and like children, are more focused when their bodies are occupied with a physical activity. I have not done this, but can imagine sitting beside a directee moulding clay with her, while listening and accompanying her journey. It is a case of us being set free by the creative spirit (and creative Spirit) to offer liberative contexts for direction.

Through the Spirit, the beyond is brought near: gifting

In the Pauline Epistles, there are two lists of gifts, in 1 Corinthians 12 and in Romans 12. In the former, they are specifically called spiritual gifts, implying that they are given to individuals by the Holy Spirit. In the latter, they are simply gifts, but again Paul implies that they come from God: 'according to the grace given to us' (Rom. 12.6). In both cases, they are given for the benefit of the new community of disciples, the Church.

These lists, like most Pauline lists, are illustrative rather than exhaustive, giving a sense of what God brings 'from beyond' into our lives in the ongoing process of creation. The Corinthian list has often been read in charismatic circles as a set of supernatural talents, but the Romans list subverts that reading. Alongside prophecy and teaching we find leading and cheerfulness. The truth is that there is no such distinction, as we have already emphasized. As an ongoing act of grace, God gives 'gifts for life', which equip us for a closer relationship with God, a more wholesome relationship with the wider community and a more creative and missional approach in the local church.

And God gives 'gifts for spiritual direction' too. These fall under the general heading of 'insight', which enables proper discernment, encourages healthy interaction (cheerfulness!), speaks and acts for the benefit of the other (wisdom) and challenges that which is not 'godly' (prophecy). Behind all of these aspects of insight lurks the key question of how that gifting is given by the Holy Spirit and accessed by us in the *here and now* of a session of direction.

THE HOLY SPIRIT AND COMPANIONSHIP

The world of charismatic Christianity to which I was introduced at university was an exhilarating one for many, a sense of release to be the person God had made us to be and a reassurance that God loved us as we were. But it also introduced us to a language of power and assurance that at times opened the door to abuse and overweening confidence. Gifts, we were told, were given to the twice-blessed by the Holy Spirit, and we could be absolutely certain that when we used them, God was speaking through us. Some began to use formulaic language to underline the fact that God was using us special vessels; 'God has told me to tell you …' was one of the most troubling. We had words of knowledge that led us to knock on particular doors, knowing that God had sent us there; words of prophecy to tell the church congregation how unregenerate it was.

If only it were so easy! The doctrine of the Holy Spirit, whatever it teaches, teaches us that we are not in control of the power of God in any sense at all. It teaches us humility! Rather, God chooses to prompt us, inspire us and guide us using the natural talents of common sense and reasoned intelligence, the cumulative wisdom of generations, the discipline and hard graft of our study and, no doubt, those mysterious serendipities and strange inklings of a world beyond. Certainly God can act directly and in an unmediated way through the Holy Spirit in our lives as spiritual directors, but it is critical that we recognize the actions of the Holy Spirit as coming through all channels of human insight, identified by a careful and often prolonged act of discernment, testing the spirits: 'To see whether they are from God' (1 John 4.1).

A simple example may help to earth this. When I give direction, I often use fragments of thoughts, prayers, readings and observations which have struck me over the recent past. As time has gone on, I have been surprised how often people have received those fragments as 'a word from the Lord', which speaks directly to their condition. There are several important features of this. The first is that I don't speak with the false arrogance of pretending to know the mind of God. The second is that when I speak, the discernment often comes from the other, the pilgrim. She it is who is best placed on the whole to know what is useful or consoling. Finally, it often seems to be in the spaces or gaps or silences that God speaks, or even in the words that the directee hears me say that I have not actually said. This is both reassuring and humbling: the Holy Spirit works in me, through me, despite me and my shortcomings, gifting me but never turning me into a fount of all spiritual wisdom.

Even here there is a danger that the spiritual director will be seen as the person with divine power, and some who ask us to accompany them would like the easy option of being told what to do. Philippians 2 gives us the counterbalance to this. True power, Paul tells us, is modelled on Jesus' complete relinquishment of control, force and ownership, on the self-emptying that takes the form of a slave, obeys the Father and gives himself away. This is redemptive power. As we imitate Christ in our work of direction, we do the same. The only power we ought to exercise is the power to pour ourselves out for the sake of the other.

Through the Spirit, the beyond is brought near: language and silence

I now return to my opening story about being 'baptized in the Holy Spirit' while at college. The theological history of the phrase is complex, going back to the Wesleyan idea of entire sanctification. As it developed, there emerged a theology of two or more baptisms: water baptism and Spirit baptism. This was accompanied by an emerging theory of hierarchies of Christians, those who were only 'water baptized' and those who were 'Spirit baptized' as well. At worst, this turns Holy Spirit back into a substance, a quantity, and gives false power to those who have more of 'it'.

THE HOLY SPIRIT AND COMPANIONSHIP

This is of course completely contrary to the New Testament understanding of baptism. Those who are baptized in the Christian Church are 'baptized into Christ' and 'filled with the Holy Spirit'. There is an outward action to this when the person is immersed in water or some variant of that, with the Trinitarian formula: 'N, I baptize you in the name of the Father and of the Son and of the Holy Spirit.' This is the sacramental sign, which points to the new life of the believer. That new life is the new life of and in the Holy Spirit.

We know that some people live their Christian lives more simply, single-mindedly and transparently, but it is a theological falsehood to suggest that different people have different percentages of the Spirit, who is a person and cannot be parcelled out. So we prefer to say that when a person is baptized the God beyond comes near, and also that the outworking of this approach takes a lifetime to unfold. This enables me now, with the distance of more than 40 years since that experience, to make theological sense of it. I was baptized at the ripe age of six months, but 21 years later, the Holy Spirit who came to me in my baptism 'popped the cork out of my bottle' or opened me up more fully to the rich, exciting and scary vulnerabilities of the Christian life. I do not therefore choose to call that experience a 'baptism', because it is theologically confusing. To reiterate what I said earlier, it is not a category of the presence of God, but an experience, an event in which I am deeply confident God continued his work in me more dramatically than is usually the case.

And what at the time was most dramatic for me and for those watching was that I began to 'speak in tongues', something that I have continued to do over the intervening years. If it was not 'proof' of a second blessing, or a climb up some supposed spiritual ladder, what was going on, and did it involve the Holy Spirit at all? The answer is that it contains three possible meanings or functions. First of all, the phenomenon of *glossolalia* is well attested in more than one religious tradition, and such spontaneous outpourings are part of the human condition. We speak like this when we are learning to talk, when we are ecstatic, sometimes in play, and often when our ability to use language deteriorates with use. It is often full of expressive meaning, though sometimes seemingly devoid of rational content. Second, it – like many other forms of speech – may be used as an expression of religious faith or response. We may choose, consciously or unconsciously, to use this sound-world as a gift of our communication with the God who is beyond us, precisely because 'normal' everyday modes of communication seem trite or unable to contain deep meaning.

The third way of reading *glossolalia* is that – with the eyes and ears and lips of faith – we regard our speaking in tongues as itself a gift of the Holy Spirit which enables us to transcend normal meaning and expression. Then we can say that the God who has given us the normal gift of verbal communication, recognizing that those words fail at times, gives us the ecstatic gift of non-rational communication, in tongues.

For those engaged in accompanying others in their spiritual journey, this enables us to propose a broader understanding of what constitutes the proper language of 'God-conversation'. The formal languages of liturgical prayer and extempore vocal prayer are sufficient for many, but to them we may add the expressive languages of 'tongues', groans, sighs, tears and laughter; the patient waiting which listening requires; and of course the apophatic 'language' of silence. In guiding those who wish to 'pray better', we can release people from the angst of thinking that they are not praying properly because they are not doing it in the way they were once taught. We can introduce people to forms of prayer that are more akin to their character or experience or current life circumstances. And we can suggest that people play with different forms of communication in their engagement with a God who delights in the richness and variety of 'The Word'.

Through the Spirit, God wells up from within, in holiness

We now turn to the theme of immanence, the idea that the Holy Spirit wells up from within us. I have always loved the Sufi saying that 'God is closer to me than my jugular vein', which reinforces Augustine of Hippo's comment that God is closer to me than I am to myself. The first work of the immanent Spirit in us is of course the work of holiness.

I have always been troubled by Christian preaching and direction that portrays God as an external 'other' who watches us like a hawk, waiting to catch us out and then pouncing on us in judgement. The burden of guilt, the sense of the impossibility of change in my life and the fear of failure all trap us in a legalistic parody of holiness which is very far from the biblical model. The apostle Paul, in the depths of a tragic controversy with the Christians of Corinth, finds enough grace to say to them that 'You show that you are a letter of Christ ... written not with ink but with the Spirit of the living God, not on tablets of stone but on tablets of human hearts' (2 Cor. 3.3). In saying this, he is building on the long prophetic tradition well captured by Jeremiah: 'This is the covenant that I will make with the house of Israel after those days, says the Lord: I will put my law within them, and I will write it on their hearts; and I will be their God, and they shall be my people' (Jer. 31.33). Both the above texts capture the idea of immanence – 'within-ness' – through their reference to the heart with which God does business. We can change, because the Holy Spirit is constantly welling up within us, writing indelibly on our lives.

This inner work of the Spirit is co-operative, and the very act of spiritual direction models this. The interplay between directee, director and Holy Spirit is one in which we are not always sure who the agent is. And of course, it is not necessary to name the agent in the journey of transformation. We are co-agents, another reminder that the directee is not a blank canvas on which the director writes the life of God.

A little illustration here may help to clarify the mechanics of transformation. It is trite, but can be easily be translated into other life contexts. There was a time when I used to drive fast and furiously, and protested that I was in 'full control' when challenged by parishioners. The pressure of their anxious care continued long enough for me to 'be convicted' by it. I have deliberately used the forensic language beloved of evangelicals so that I can subvert it. My parishioners didn't convict me, but their thoughtful concern broke through my arrogance, and the first step to change was my willingness to hear criticism, the prophetic voice of the Holy Spirit.

The second step was my futile attempt to pull myself together, and the more I tried, the more I failed. The consequence was despair, turning into prayer, 'Lord, if you would have me change, then you must make the change happen.' While this sounds passive, it is actually the second step in the process, calling the Holy Spirit into co-agency with me. In this sense, no prayer is passive.

The third step was the painful slow waiting. In this case, I quite forgot about my prayer until I noticed after 18 months that I was driving more slowly than usual. I tried to speed up and scared the living daylights out of myself. Since then, I have (mostly) been more measured, and wish that all the other things I would like changed in me were quite so easy! But I find it helpful to walk with the Holy Spirit towards changed life through active listening, praying, waiting, and from time to time, celebrating. Change is possible. God is within us. The task of the spiritual director is to help articulate this and to share in the process as another part of the divine agency in change.

Through the Spirit, God wells up from within, in prayer

The one thing that is problematic with my illustration is that it might encourage a 'list' mentality in the pursuit of holiness, striving towards a series of stepped moral changes. Having grown up with the traditional checklists of sins to go through before entering the confessional, I'm very aware of the danger of this. The key clue in the illustration is the reference to prayer. The pursuit of holiness is at heart the pursuit of a growing relationship with God. To live well is to live 'in tune' with God.

Continuing the musical metaphor, in order to live in tune with God, we need to allow the music of the Spirit to play within our spirits. That music arises from many sources: scripture, community both Christian and human, the cosmos itself. Some people hear it in deeply personal experiences, through their dreams or intuitions, in passing conversations. Controversially, not a few Christians hear it through what have come to be known as psychic events as well. The simple first point is that God wells up from within us without let or hindrance when we are good, active, practised listeners, trained in attunement, recognition and participation. These are the disciplines that help us to stand aside and open us up to the sound of the Holy Spirit in our lives.

1 Attunement

Another personal illustration may help. I used to wonder how bird watchers saw birds where I only saw bushes. Now I understand that they have their eyes on 'fixed focus' in the middle distance, attuned to particular small movements, believing that there are nearly always birds to be seen where there are bushes. Translating this into the world of spiritual attunement, we are encouraged (and encourage others) to have our eyes on 'God focus', believing that the Holy Spirit is constantly welling up from within, through the media of scripture, community, cosmos and experience. There is also a danger here. Just as the twitcher may miss the bird not in the normal place, so we may limit the media through which we will allow the Holy Spirit to make music. Those from an evangelical tradition may be nervous of allowing non-scriptural sounds to sing the song of God, while those from a liberal tradition may do the same with scripture! Culturally, Africans assume that the Holy Spirit sings into our dreams, but a Western reading of dreams tells us more about our love of Freud than our love of God. As spiritual directors, we have our own cultural and theological boundaries and limitations, but we too must be open to the variety of voices with which the Holy Spirit speaks.

The key in all of this is that the doctrine of the Holy Spirit teaches us that the God does not respect any boundaries that we put in place:

> What is born of the flesh is flesh, and what is born of the Spirit is spirit. Do not be astonished that I said to you, 'You must be born from above.' The wind blows where it chooses, and you hear the sound of it, but you do not know where it comes from or where it goes. So it is with everyone who is born of the Spirit. (John 3.6–8)

Attunement begins when our working hypothesis is that God, who is always present, might in any given situation be singing to us.

2 Recognition

But of course, we may be deluded! The counterfoil to our over-positive statement is that God's might not be the voice that we are hearing. A little discrimination is needed lest we create a god out of our own wishful thinking. Having once spent ten minutes watching an airborne scarecrow in the sure conviction that it was a rare raptor, I know this temptation well. Recognition demands discernment. Ignatius of Loyola spoke in this regard of consolations and desolations: consolations are for him 'those intellectual insights, emotional impulses, invitations, or pulls that led him to love God more deeply and to desire whatever God desires'. Desolations are 'the various forms of intellectual darkness that led him to deny the will of God' (Burke-Sullivan and Burke, 2009, loc. 583). The fruit or outcome of our supposed recognition of the presence and the voice of God will bear the gospel characteristic of love. Of course, we need to be alert to the self-deception of 'desolate consolations', those movements that superficially seem to reflect love but ultimately bear the mark of self-love. And conversely, we recognize that consolations may themselves be painful or troubling at first sight, and that there are therefore 'consolate desolations', struggles and difficulties which lead us towards God (we noted these in detail in the last chapter when thinking about the cross).

3 Participation

The third discipline of listening is participation, the act of joining in with the wider communion of saints in prayerful reflection. In the next two chapters, we will look at the cumulative wisdom of the Christian Scriptures and the tradition of the Church, which give us confidence in a history of shared listening. Similarly, the act of seeking spiritual direction has at its core the assumption that two are better at listening than one. Living in an age in which spiritual conversation has become privatized and individualized, the idea that we might talk to each other about how and when we hear God has become a marginal activity, for contemplatives and dreamers. The recovery of the discipline of spiritual direction needs to include the practice of shared spiritual conversation in cells and groups. This of course is why Jesus says in one of the few gospel passages on the idea of the Church: 'For where two or three are gathered in my name, I am there among them' (Matt. 18.20).

Through the Spirit, God wells up from within, and drives us out

The third act of the Spirit within is missional, driving us back into the world. It is the ultimate antidote to the selfish spiritual desire to be safe, withdrawn, disengaged, and it is Jesus' prayer in John 17. Though we, his disciples, do not belong to the world, we belong *in* the world, sent by the Spirit just as Jesus was. This missional driving out is the central theme of the Acts of the Apostles. Intriguingly, this takes us back to where we began this chapter, with my experience of 'speaking in tongues.' On every occasion in Acts when a group (always a group) of disciples speaks in tongues or receives the Holy Spirit, or both, the gospel is preached to a new people group: first the Jews gathered from the Diaspora in Jerusalem for Pentecost (Acts 2), then among the Samaritans (Acts 8), then notably in Saul's conversion (Acts 9 – the making of the apostle to the Gentiles), reinforced in Peter's vision and preaching in chapter 10. Finally, Paul meets Ephesian followers of John the Baptist and lays hands on them: 'the Holy Spirit came upon them, and they spoke in tongues and prophesied. Altogether there were about twelve of them' (Acts 19.6–7). Isn't it striking that when the Holy Spirit acts in this way, a new group of apostles/disciples is formed, a twelve, a new church!

Then too this Spirit of mission is a stirrer, stirring up not trouble but compassion. The model for this is Jesus himself. At the beginning of his ministry in Luke's Gospel, Jesus uses the model of liberative compassion in Isaiah 61 as his blueprint for the mission of the kingdom of God. Once engaged in that mission, Jesus' repeated response to the needs of individuals and communities is one of a heart stirred in anguish and sometimes anger to active compassion. We might say that the Holy Spirit who drives us out is the one who forms our vocation to be the people of God in the world.

This means that a key part of the director's task is to help directees see the world as God sees it, ache over the world with the compassion of God, and respond as Jesus would. To accompany others is to lead them into their true vocation as '*alter Christus*', Christ's heart and hands active today in the world.

Reflection and questions

- Some of us find it difficult to admit to our gifts. To get around this, you might like to write a prayer or a poem celebrating who you are and what you are gifted at in a constructive act of celebration and thanksgiving. How might this be a useful exercise in direction itself?

- One of the themes of this chapter is that the Holy Spirit brings the beyond near, and also wells up from within. Which of these two verbal images best reflects your own experience, and how might you receive the other image as a challenge to grow spiritually? Do you notice these movements also in directing and being directed and, if so, how do they manifest themselves?

- Attunement to the presence of the Spirit needs working at. Set yourself the task for a day (or longer) to ask what signs of God's presence there are. What is your practice here and how does your daily practice of attunement relate to what happens in a direction session where you are also looking for God's presence?

- Think through the names, images and metaphors which you use for God. How many of them are loaded with a gender bias? Is there a need in your own thought and conversation for a shift to begin to occur? How might this best be raised within a direction relationship?

6

Theological Approaches to the Bible in Accompaniment

If you, the reader, have stayed with us to this point in our book we hope you will have noticed our emphasis first and foremost in our practical theology of spiritual direction on the presence and activity of God, the community of the Three-In-One. We have explored this as fully as we can, given the finite space there is in a book of this nature. In this chapter and the next we move, as it were, to another level. We address human-divine (or divine-human) supports for the work of companionship through the use of the Bible and the Christian Tradition as it has developed over the centuries. We begin with addressing the place of the Bible in spiritual companionship.

It has become current and helpful when discussing practical theology to employ the 'theology in four voices' approach (Cameron *et al*, 2010, pp. 53–6):

1. Operant Voice: theology embedded within the actual practices of a group.
2. Espoused Voice: theology embedded within a group's articulation of its beliefs.
3. Normative Voice: scripture; creeds; official teachings and liturgies of the Church.
4. Formal Voice: theology of 'professional' trained theologians; dialogue with other disciplines.

While we could have created the whole book around this

approach it is only *an* approach and we introduce it at this point as a way of helpfully framing this chapter for several reasons (and perhaps the reader can see how we have moved somewhat between these four voices in the earlier material). We employ this way of working here because there are some very good existing materials covering both normative and formal theology around the use of the Bible in pastoral practice and spiritual direction which do not need repetition here. The first of these is Liz Hoare's comprehensive treatment *Using the Bible in Spiritual Direction*. Hoare's book actually goes further than its title suggests in my view and describes a whole way of being a spiritual director out of interaction with the Bible as a foundation for all that companionship is. Second are two books from a series creating dialogue around the Bible and pastoral practice which have borne the test of time. Gordon Oliver addresses all the major questions of both critical biblical scholarship and grounded working with the scriptural text in his *Holy Bible, Human Bible: Questions Pastoral Practice Must Ask*. Related to this is an important book of internationally sourced essays edited by Paul Ballard and Stephen Holmes, *The Bible in Pastoral Practice: Readings in the Place and Function of Scripture in the Church*.

We will refer to these works from time to time but I want to start this chapter in a different place by describing the operant and espoused theology that emerges from my actual practice of using the Bible in spiritual direction. I fully recognize that this is a particular personal starting point and that I might not be able to see some things that I do in my operant theology that don't fully square with my espoused theology, but that is again why Hoare's book and supervision are so important – as correctives to the many things I may be missing. The reader as directee and/or director may then be able to repeat the exercise for themselves in useful ways.

There are several occasions when the Bible appears in my

practice of companionship. A directee may bring a scripture text they have been working with in their prayer and we may wrestle with its meaning and how it might stand both for us and over against us. A particular topic of conversation arising from an initial narrated experience may elicit a question something like, 'Which Bible text or story do you most associate with what we've been talking about?' Often, but not every time, I offer the reading of a relevant and apt Bible text as an appropriate 'boundary' to the session. Occasionally I may suggest a text to see if it 'fits' with the directee's experience; we may practise a meditation with it or they may take it away with them to pray through before next time. Sometimes the same text arises multiple times. It is also possible that a whole direction session may go by without a mention of a particular scripture at all.

What does this practice say about my operant theology? At least four topics emerge quite quickly:

1. It looks as though the Bible (or at least certain chosen texts within the Bible) is an important, though not strictly necessary, resource and even a theological authority within which to understand, encourage and perhaps challenge the experience of any directee.
2. The text is somehow 'alive' (the living Word, animated by God the Spirit?), relevant and able to 'speak' in the 'here and now' of any particular companionship conversation.
3. There is some kind of theological correlation between the 'text'[15] which the experience of the directee evokes and the text of the chosen scripture. This goes much beyond a 'this = that' kind of equation to a subtle and sophisticated relationship which needs explication.
4. For such practice to be coherent over time and not just

---

15 Amongst several theorists of experiential practice, any event, narrative or material artefact can be treated as 'text': something to be investigated and interpreted.

random matching, there is in the background a 'bigger picture' or universal theological narrative within which each particular text is fitted and understood.

Thus we have the agenda for this chapter, which will move through an espousing of theology for the use of the Bible in the companionship room while drawing regularly on more formal and normative approaches.

Where does the Bible 'fit' in spiritual direction?

Knowledge of the Bible and its contents is presented here in my operant theology as an assumption that is brought to direction by both the pilgrim and the accompanier. Perhaps, however, this is not always the case with every directee, and with a perceived decline in 'biblical literacy' it may not be tenable in the longer term. I would suggest though with Liz Hoare that it is very difficult to imagine a director being fully rounded in their practice without a working knowledge of the Bible (2015, p. 10). What kind of authority the Bible has in the direction session is a question raised by this practice.

To simplify things somewhat there are two chief ways in which Christians have approached this question. The first is to say that the Bible stands as *the* source of authority above all others for our faith and practice. The alternative view is that the Bible is *a* vital and irreducible source for us alongside our experience, reason and the Tradition of the Church. This latter approach may place the Bible as the final arbiter in any dialogue between the different sources (as in the so-called Wesleyan Quadrilateral of the Methodist Church) or place it on equal terms with the Tradition (since, so the argument goes, the Tradition flows directly from the source of the Scriptures).

We will not resolve these questions in a few paragraphs here, but we will wrestle with them a bit further. Once again, though, it is important to note that nothing in the practice of the Church over the centuries ignores or bypasses the Bible in any way.

The Anglican 'normative theology' set out clearly in the *39 Articles* (Article VI) is that 'Holy Scripture containeth all things necessary to salvation.' Oliver helpfully explicates the Bible as container (2006, pp. 32–6). He points out that the metaphor of container is not being used here in the sense that a can contains only tomato soup. Rather the Bible is a container for a whole mixture of things which may have different uses at different times. This leaves us with a spiritual discernment task about using the Bible – we can't use it all. In our operant theology, there is always our personal (or our church's) 'canon within the canon' or, to put it crudely, our favourite bits. As we have seen, in my experience, this is how the Bible is used in spiritual direction – a text is sought, sometimes chosen, often gifted and this suffices for the moment of discernment.

In developing a formal theology Oliver then cites three ways in which the Bible is laid alongside a) our experience of God in the natural world, b) the Christian Tradition (as equal partners) in Roman Catholic and Orthodox Churches, and c) God 'speaking' or revealing Godself through other religions (from St Paul's multi-cultural world to today's). The continuity here is once again the activity of God. As Oliver remarks, the assumption of the compilers of the *39 Articles*

> was that God's character guarantees that God's true speaking through nature, the properly based traditions of the Church, and other faiths will always be consonant with God's speaking in the Bible. (2006, p. 34)

We will develop this theme further in the next section but it is worth quoting Oliver's conclusion on the question of authority:

> The authority of the Bible derives from God whose word it

contains, and from the solidarity of present day Christians with the early communities of believers who collected, edited and wrote it, not from some quasi-magical quality of the text itself. (p. 35)

Speaking of a 'quasi-magical' quality brings to mind what is known as the 'proof-texting' method of using the Bible, still prevalent in some parts of our Churches. Here a verse or two of scripture is employed like a 'bible bullet' either to shoot down a particular argument or to reinforce a viewpoint. The text is taken out of context and often loses any connection with its original meaning. There is no meeting of person and text, no mutual interaction, no space with which to explore and challenge. We will return to seeing the parts in the whole of the Bible later in the chapter.

One final development of the container metaphor beloved of the Anglican Reformers is a communitarian one. Oliver offers the picture of a country or nation as a container of peoples with many internal differences and boundaries between them which requires: 'A shared sense of freedom, openness, opportunity, interaction' (p. 35) if it is to thrive. So working with the Bible as a source of authority is like going to another country. There will be a 'push and pull' towards and away from the stranger. Both sides will need to accommodate and assimilate to the new situation in order that they can meet. Comfort, agreement, challenge and dialogue can move both ways. Oliver extends the idea of the hospitality of Scripture later in the book and I think it is a fruitful area since spiritual direction, at some basic level, is an act of hospitality on the part of director and directee. Here is a great description of what a brief interaction around a Bible text might mean:

> The stranger [the chosen text] comes from a distance, stays around for a while for a purpose, then continues on their

journey. The one who is received with hospitality, however generously, retains their otherness, their own integrity. The guest may certainly make their presence felt, but after they have continued on their way, the host is left to reflect on what has changed that would not have changed otherwise as a result of the encounter, and to reflect on what will stay different as a result of what has been said, shared, argued about, explored. (p. 124)

One of the tasks of the director then in relation to the Bible is to create the space where such resourceful hospitality with the Bible can take place.

The Living Word in spiritual direction

One of the Bible texts that is often rolled out in relation to how the Bible understands itself is 2 Timothy 3.16, which states that every scripture (literally text or writing) is God-breathed or 'inspired by God'. Of course this can take us down the route of equating the Word of God with the Bible (rather than the Bible containing the Word as we have seen) but it does give us another theological hook with which to think about how the Bible operates in spiritual direction – that of inspiration.

Inspiration and breathing direct us to the breath of God, the Holy Spirit who was 'hovering over the waters' at creation, who breathed life into Adam (Gen. 2.7) and was the breath and wind animating the apostles after the resurrection of Jesus (John 20.22; Acts 2.2). And the Spirit continues to be the creative energy and life flowing as God from God – living out the Spirit's full and equal personhood of the Godhead as we learnt in the last chapter. Placing such an understanding alongside 2 Timothy 3.16 makes the Bible a 'both and' document. Just as Oliver names his book *Holy Bible, Human Bible,* we can understand our sacred Scriptures as both written by people like us and at one and the same time inspired by the creative Spirit of God.

I like to think of the Bible therefore as a bit like Jesus. In Chapter 3 we saw how Jesus has been understood by the Church to be both fully human and fully divine. There is a sense then in which the same is true of the Bible – it is formed and forged in the messiness and difficulty of life on earth in which God is still at work. And God by the Spirit has gifted us these human Scriptures which have been chosen to be God's word for us. Approaching the Scriptures as God's word is an act and stance of faith. This and only this is what sets them apart from any other literature for the Christian; that they are inspired by the one and same Spirit who was present at creation and realizes our salvation.

Therefore just as Jesus the incarnate one overturns lots of expectations about what it is to be human and fully open to God and the activity of the Spirit in his own day, so the Bible too constantly disturbs our comfortable lives in our day. Oliver states this view clearly at the start of his book, comparing Scripture to being

> more like a caged animal, restless to be set free to disrupt and challenge the assumptions of its hearers, than like a pet animal that has become a kind of lifestyle accessory for Christians who happen to value it. (p. 1)

If we take this line of thought further, that the Bible is inspired by God, then there is a sense in which just as we live *inside* of God, the Three-In-One (as we noted in Chapter 3) the Bible joins us as another companion in that space. God as we have also remarked has 'all the time in the world' and we notice the in-breaking of eternity when we are in the 'flow' of what God is up to in a '*kairos*' moment with a pilgrim. And here we come to an important understanding of how the Bible operates in spiritual direction.

The animation of the written word by the Holy Spirit makes using the Bible a *here and now* event – part of that spring of living waters bubbling up within each believer moment by moment. In treating the text this way we move from a *'there and then'* approach which only studies the text as an inanimate object to understanding its nature as a living thing (Oliver's caged animal set free) in the moment. This is the same move that the theoreticians of interpretation recommend we make if we are to recover a sense of being 'in front of the text' from a position that we are much more used to of being 'behind the text'.[16] As Oliver shows, we disregard historical criticism of the Bible at our peril (pp. 11–12, cf. the earlier comment about proof-texting), but this leaves us with what can easily become a dead letter being picked apart.

We can think of it like this. The Bible is like a play enacted in a theatre. The place where it truly comes alive is in front of the stage when it is being performed. All sorts of things have to go on 'behind the scenes' for the play to happen and they are important, but the action is in the front of the stage not behind it. It is probably fair to say we have spent a bit too long in the past few centuries peering into the darker corners of the storerooms in the theatre of the Bible rather than making the text alive in the *here and now* of a performance.

Much of prayer practice creates the ability in the one praying to be present – attentive to the *here and now*. Theologically this is because God is present *where we are*, not where we imagine God to be (e.g. in past experiences or an imagined future when we have sorted out all the things that get in the way of being fully open to God!). It is no surprise then that many of the prayer practices that utilize the Bible as a starting point, such as the Benedictines' *Lectio Divina* (Hoare, 2015, pp. 79–83)

---

16 For a fuller explanation of this hermeneutical theory see Craig Bartholomew's chapter entitled 'In Front of the Text: the quest of hermeneutics' in Ballard and Holmes, eds, 2005, pp. 135–52.

and the Jesuits' imagining of the Gospel texts (pp. 83–9), place the one praying squarely in front of the text. The Holy Spirit as inspirer of the word and the Christian reading make the written word alive in the *here and now*. The same is happening I believe in my practice of companionship when I use the Bible as described earlier; I and the pilgrim find ourselves in front of the text, and in its performance, to return to our analogy, we can be confronted in fresh and inspiring ways by God's Spirit animating the written word.

Perhaps this point is better made by describing the difference between the written and spoken word. As Oliver (pp. 23ff) points out, in much of the Bible, for most of the history of the Church and for many lay Christians even today the Bible has been a spoken word which is heard in public (not least because as St Paul tells us in Rom. 10.17 'faith comes by hearing'). The speaking of the text is by definition a *here and now* event – it will be slightly different from when it was heard yesterday and perhaps even more surprising when listened to tomorrow, even if the same text is read aloud again and again. Reading and studying the written word privately, while equally important, is simply not in the same category.[17] Thus the quasi-liturgical ending of a companionship meeting by the reading aloud of a text that has been significant in the conversation leads to a further element of formal theology around the Bible in direction – understanding it as a *sacrament*.

Oliver introduces this idea following an article in a journal by Stephen Wright and it properly extends the 'here and nowness' of Scripture into a 'transcendental moment of encounter'. As described by Oliver a sacrament is

a kind of open container within which the drama of holy

---

17 I have just changed email and website support companies. The new provider has a name that reads a bit like an ethnic Middle Eastern restaurant, since it is spelt in a colloquial way, but when read out loud it is obvious that the aim of the company is to 'ease your technology problems'.

words and of divine and human actions are held together. It is also an 'effective action' in the technical sense that it is intended to deliver what it symbolises. (p. 36)

Sacraments are bigger on the inside as it were (a bit like Doctor Who's time machine, The Tardis) – there is mystery and intrigue about them and they are very difficult to explain. In fact we shouldn't really attempt an explanation at all.

Thus when we say 'This is the Word of the Lord' at the end of a public reading we are opening up the sacramental container of Scripture to all sorts of possibilities. I do wonder, however, whether the shorter version, simply, 'The Word of the Lord', does not leave open an even wider interpretive door. It is easier, I think, to put a question mark at the end of 'The Word of the Lord?' and thus open up the hearer to a spirit of inquiry about the text, especially when it is one of the tougher or more obscure texts that seem strange to our ears.

The sacramental nature of Scripture also helps us with its use in understanding how so-called 'prayer words' operate in contemplative prayer. It is recommended by some practitioners of this tradition that a word of Scripture is chosen and repeated (e.g. *maranatha*, 'even so come', in the John Main school). Or think of the Orthodox Jesus Prayer: 'Lord Jesus Christ, Son of the Living God, have mercy on me, a sinner'. It is based on at least three scriptures: assertions of Jesus as Lord in, for example, Philippians 2; the annunciation reference to Jesus as Son of God (especially Luke 1.35); and the prayer of the publican in Luke 18.13. Repeated endlessly time after time these words become a whole new kind of sacramental container for inner silence. It's also true that some charismatic worship turns, after a time of singing particular songs, to repetitive, even contemplative use of particular words drawn from Scripture, particularly names for God and Jesus. A new kind of communitarian worshipful space emerges for the participants at such moments.

The sacramental nature of the Bible in relating how the words become the Word takes us directly to our next section in that, as Oliver points out, the Bible

> has to be able to hold together possibilities of comparisons and parallels between Scripture and the experience of the hearer with possibilities of contrast, confusion and mystery. In the Bible Christians find many passages that offer comparisons and parallels between the experience of the writers and their own experiences. (2006, p. 37)

Correlating the Bible and our experience

As we saw when describing my operant theology of the Bible in spiritual direction, often it is laid alongside a story, experience or conversation in several different ways. So we now turn to discussing a more formal theologizing that arises from this way of working. Elaine Graham, Heather Walton and Frances Ward describe seven 'methods' of theological reflection in their book of that title. At least two of their methods are relevant here and those wishing to delve further might like to consult the relevant chapters; 'Speaking of God in Public': Correlation; 'Speaking in Parables': Constructive Narrative Theology. Much of the material in this section is drawn from this source.

Turning to 'Speaking of God in Public' first then, Christianity, since the earliest and shortest Christian Creed which declared 'Jesus is Lord' (1 Cor. 12.3), has been a public religion. In a world where the Roman Emperor, often named the Caesar, was described as 'Lord' or *Kyrios* in Greek it is no wonder that Christians were variously laughed at (see e.g. Acts 17.32) and then persecuted for their rival claim. Ever since those times the Church has had to find ways of speaking about God in public such that our voice might be heard. In the twentieth century a whole way of doing theology arose around the notion of 'correlation' from Paul Tillich, David Tracy and others. Essentially, but perhaps oversimplifying the case, the argument is that God has made all that there is and so it is possible to draw on all sources of human knowledge, particularly the so-called 'new' human sciences of psychology and psychotherapy, for the creating of theological understanding. It is an argument we have made from the start of this book. While there are critics of this approach who wish to assert the primacy of Christian theology, it has allowed practical methods of discerning the activity of God in the wider world beyond the Church in helpful ways. It also allows an important 'two-way street' to develop so that Christian theology and its traditions including the Bible can be critiqued from the 'outside' (which remains inside the whole created order). The method is best exemplified by the interactive triangle of Bible and Tradition, current human experience and cultural information (from multiple sources) championed by Whitehead and Whitehead in *Method in Ministry* (see also Graham, Walton and Ward, 2005, p. 161).

A really great example of this method put into action (I have no idea whether this is conscious or not) is found in Belden Lane's *The Solace of Fierce Landscapes*. Lane combines his experience of accompanying his mother to her death with an exploration of the references to the prayer of the desert and the mountain in the Bible and the Tradition alongside wisdom from psychology, all within a movement through purgation, illumination and union. It occurs to us that utilizing the Bible in such a correlative way fills it out and releases Oliver's caged animal in a safe and fruitful manner and we commend the method for spiritual directors and their companions alike.

The second way in which correlation occurs is via the imagination, which Graham, Walton and Ward note was added in by Whitehead as an important modification to his method (2005, p. 162). I have written elsewhere about how the imagination can be recovered as an important approach to reflecting theologically

(Rooms, 2011, pp. 61–5). The full method is described by Graham, Walton and Ward as 'Speaking in Parables' and utilizes story and metaphor in correlative and creative ways.

Experiences which are narrated, metaphors which arise from them and Bible stories all create imaginative 'worlds' which can be inhabited for a while and played with – playfulness is important here in creative spiritual direction. They can be laid alongside each other, interrogate each other and so offer mutual comfort and critique. Transformation in the Christian life is about moving from the world I currently occupy to a new, liberative and fruitful world and using narrative and metaphor can really shift things. It is also possible to get stuck in our stories and images so remembering the aim is transformation will be essential for directors using this method.

Perhaps this can be best explained with an example from my own life. Several years ago now, I was in the midst of my mid-life 'transition', as I came to call it (I prefer transition to 'crisis' as I've never much admired middle-aged men in sports cars!). On retreat I was imagining myself, using the Ignatian method of biblical meditation, with Jesus at the wedding at Cana (John 2). I sat down with Jesus at a table (they had tables then in my imagining!) and he offered me a glass of the [best] wine he had just made. I refused it. This imaginative experience pushed me back to formative experiences of somehow not wanting the best for myself and asked the question as to whether I could now seek God's best, whatever that might be in the second half of my life. I spent several subsequent years working with this text and the images and worlds it created until a 'best' future began to emerge.

Our story and the bigger story in the whole Bible

So far we have examined the use of Scripture in companionship by thinking about how individual texts and narratives are used. But what about the bigger picture, the whole story? The Bible comes to us as a collection of individual books and many different genres as well as a whole with some overarching story to tell. Unless as directors and directees we have some sense of this bigger story we may, literally, 'lose the plot' as we shall see.[18]

Sam Wells really helps us here when he discusses Scripture as narrative in relation to his project of creating Christian ethical stances (2004, pp. 53ff – we touched on this in Chapter 1). He picks up a suggestion of N. T. Wright which describes the whole Bible as a kind of five act play where the fifth act is missing and is to be completed by the Church working out what happens as it goes along.[19] Wells likes the overall idea but modifies it significantly and, in my view, helpfully. Let me summarize here his overview of the whole Bible.

The first act is creation in Genesis 1—11 and (disagreeing with Wright) this includes humanity walking away from the original blessing and order of creation with the increasing horror of Genesis 3—11. In fact, as Wells points out, all the first four acts have elements of glory and horror between God's activity and the human response. The calling of Israel is the second act described as a 'love story' where God's promise and faithfulness in the covenant is sometimes received as vocation with joy by the nation of Israel and sometimes is rejected. It is important for Wells that Jesus is in the centre of the story in the middle act – act three. Here the author of the whole drama enters the fray and we know the horror and the glory that follows. Thus is the Church created in the fourth unfinished act and is given all

---

18 Some readers might be interested to compare what we say here with another of Graham, Walton and Ward's methods of theological reflection: Canonical Narrative Theology (see pp. 78-108). This would give us three suggestive approaches to Scripture from these methods: the correlative triangle, the inspired imagination and the 'intersectionality' of a text with the whole biblical narrative and our place in it.
19 This is a slightly different use of the dramatic 'play' metaphor than the one we used earlier to illustrate being 'in front of the text.'

the resources she needs in the sacraments and once again the question is will she be faithful to her vocation in the world. We know so often she is not and has not. The final fifth act is the *eschaton* or the fulfilment of the original promise at the end of all time. Christians therefore live 'between the times' – the time of the first coming of Christ and the second.

Wells shows how it is easy to think we are in any of the acts other than the one we actually inhabit, as well as not understanding our place in that one correctly. Here then is the connection with spiritual direction, given how companions often present themselves. First by being in the fourth 'in-between' act and realizing that truth for us liberates us from the need to live up to some impossible ideal of human fulfilment – trying all the time to be effective and successful as if there were only a one-act play and not one consisting of five acts. Rather we are free to experiment and fail because the future is in God's hands not ours. Faithfulness not success is required, which is 'effectiveness measured against a much longer timescale' (2004, p. 55). How many directees come to companionship exhausted from the efforts they have been making to save themselves, the Church, the world around them?

It's possible to be in the 'wrong' act in the sense that we behave in ways that show we don't really believe we are in act four at all. Thus we are not in act one or act five as the creators or finishers of the story on our own. We do not and cannot replace God, but many of us attempt to do so. If we end up sacrificing others or even ourselves (and many of us again act this out) we're in act two and living as if Jesus has not yet come as the one who ends all sacrifice. Neither are we to replace Jesus as if our job was not to find the initial resources for feeding the five thousand but to enact the miracle as Jesus. No, all the most significant things that we need have been concluded. However long we have left until act five, we are free to join in with what God continues to do since the whole story belongs to God. Wells' conclusion to his study is worth repeating here, especially if we have the lives of discipleship of ourselves and our pilgrims in mind:

> Baptism takes the Christian from a one-act play to a five-act play. In baptism, Christians are taken into a drama, where God has created them and others for a purpose, where Israel has answered a call and pursued a vocation, where Jesus has become one like them and has conquered sin and death, where the Spirit has empowered the church to follow Christ, and where God will end the drama when he sees fit. Christians find their character by becoming a character in God's story. They move from trying to realize all meaning in their own lives to receiving the heritage of faith and the hope of glory. They move from fearing their fate to singing of their destiny. For this is the effect of God's story: it transforms fate into destiny. (2004, p. 57)

Conclusion

In this chapter we have examined theologically the place of the Bible in spiritual direction. We started with actual practice which opened out four areas of exploration. We have emphasized the Bible's foundational role which is best placed alongside and in conversation with other sources as a 'container' of the Word of the Lord. The Bible is animated by the Spirit in the here and now of any direction session and has a 'public' role when spoken out loud. We have taken seriously both the particular and the universal within the Bible as a written word knowing that each has its part to play. We are ready then to add in a treatment of the Christian tradition that sits together with the Bible as a further resource for spiritual directors.

Reflection and questions

- Spend some time describing your own 'operant theology' from your actual practice of how you see the Bible being used in companionship (as a companion and a pilgrim).

- What is your espoused theology of the Bible in direction – what authority does it have? Are there places where your operant and espoused theology don't match up?

- When has the Bible most 'spoken' in a spiritual direction session for you? What happened and how did you feel? What created the conditions for such a moment? How might the experience inform your future practice?

- What is the one thing you might do differently with the Bible in companionship after reading this chapter?

- Which act of the five acts of Scripture do you find yourself most tempted to be in other than act four? What is the effect on you of being in this place and how might you move to being back in the 'in-between' times once again?

7

Spiritual Direction and the Traditions of Christianity

Here we move from the Bible to utilizing examples from the history of the Church to help us find a 'useful future in our past' to add to our understanding of what happens in companionship. The traditions which we use as examples are not rigid or prescriptive. Rather, they illustrate the centrality of spiritual direction over the centuries and some of its key recurring themes. The chapter is not an invitation to us to re-inhabit the past as traditionalists, but to draw on the living faith of the past to inform our journeys of exploration and freedom towards a living God. As Jaroslav Pelikan (1923–2006) is quoted as saying: 'Tradition is the living faith of the dead, traditionalism is the dead faith of the living' (1984, p. 65).

Introduction

In 1146 the abbess Hildegard of Bingen (1098–1197) settled down to write a letter to Bernard of Clairvaux (1090–1153) from her cloister at Mount St Disibod in Germany's Rhineland. It was her first letter, emerging from a world of complete enclosure, appealing for ecclesiastical approval of visionary experiences given her since early childhood. The church politics need not detain us, and we know how far Hildegard's travels and influence took her in later life. What is instructive for us is that Hildegard says that up to now she has told no one of these visions, 'with the single exception of a certain monk in whose exemplary life

I have the utmost confidence' (Baird, 2006, loc. 217). This was Volmar, a priest and longstanding friend of Hildegard, who was privy to her inner life, secretary for her work and business, and corrector of her Latin infelicities!

Hildegard goes on to say that 'I have, in fact, revealed all my secrets to this man, and he has given me consolation, for these are great and fearsome matters' (2006, loc. 230). This is a classic description of the role of the spiritual director, who in Hildegard's case would have been her confessor as well. He is a shadowy figure, and it is right that we know much more about her than about him (we will note more about the proper hiddenness of the director in the next chapter). Volmar stands in the shadows both of her towering mission and of the work of the Holy Spirit in her life. Vitally important to her (and to the impact of her writings, research and music), he is not important *in himself*. Rather, he is a catalyst for spiritual maturing.

Bernard's brief but encouraging reply to the letter gives us an additional taste of the practice of spiritual support and guidance which has so often come in the form of letters: 'We most earnestly urge and beseech you to recognize this gift as grace and to respond eagerly to it with all humility and devotion' (loc. 251).

The growth and development of spiritual direction

In the exchange between Hildegard and Bernard, brokered by Volmar, we discern a human and God-given instinct to seek support, guidance and spiritual wisdom from those we think wiser than ourselves. Whether the spiritual guide is actually wiser than the one she guides is a moot point. How is wisdom to be quantified anyway? Realism and humility point us in a different direction: what we offer is simply the gift of ourselves, our particular insights and experience, and the mutuality within which the Holy Spirit is able to introduce the wisdom of God.

SPIRITUAL DIRECTION AND CHRISTIANITY

Inevitably, then, we can find this instinct at work from the earliest days of Christianity, in the disciples being guided by Jesus on their travels, through the letters of Paul, to the exilic visions of John on the island of Patmos, which gave birth to a series of seven classic letters of spiritual direction to congregations in Asia Minor. As the Church grew and developed, the practice of accompaniment grew with it, though approaches have been as diverse as contexts. Variously formal and informal in delivery, it is a Christian commonplace that disciples do not and should not rely on themselves alone for the faith journey.

In the examples which follow, we are not trying to sketch a history of spiritual direction. That task has been ably fulfilled by many writers, in collections of writings and sayings like the *Philokalia* of Eastern Orthodoxy, as well as in summaries of the history like Kenneth Leech's chapter in *Soul Friend* (Chapter 2). What the collections and histories demonstrate is the fact that spiritual direction has always been an integral part of Christian *praxis*, that it is rooted in the *theoria* of our theology, and is a fundamental part of the *poiesis* or work of the community of Christian people.

So the stories we tell of previous practice, in often very different settings, emphasize the normality and centrality of spiritual direction in Christian discipleship. It isn't an add-on for privileged people. The particular illustrations we have chosen point to particular characteristics of direction that inform present practice and its underlying theological principles. They are examples of good practice, but they do not hold any special authority over us. It is not the special holiness of the director which commends her, but her faithfulness to the ways in which God reaches out to us.

Monastic lessons

The first example lies in the rise of the monastic tradition at the end of the first age of persecution, the so-called 'white martyrdom' of those who, instead of giving their blood (in 'red' martyrdom) gave their lives over to a total asceticism. In both its eremitic or solitary and community forms, the monastic ideal gave the Church a rigorous model of spiritual formation that has never left us. The twin dangers of the model are its idealization (unless you join, you're a second-class Christian) and its demonization (people who live a radical version of the faith are cut off from the world or impossibly eccentric). What was and is key to the movement down the ages is its demonstration of the need to be all or nothing as a follower of Jesus.

As someone who has never aspired to the monastic life, but whose father was a monk for 20 years, I have long known that the Benedictine way of living in the world was embedded in me before I knew myself, and that this has been a lifelong formative element of my Christian faith. One aspect of that formation has been a deeply held sense of obedience to the community and its way of life, its Rule. Being a Christian doesn't depend entirely on me. While I do need to work at my faith, it's more important to know myself carried by the community whose (sometimes petty) regulations are part of the house rules. They do me a world of good even when they seem pretty silly on the surface.

From the second century CE, Egyptian Christians began to move into the desert to live solitary lives of rigorous and ascetic prayer. Many followed them, seeking their wisdom. We know that these early hermits were rarely left alone to their solitary battles. In emergent communities, the idea of the novitiate and the novice guardian built into the emerging structure of these communities the principle of 'teacherly' accompaniment with supervision, formal discipline and a desire to imitate. It might fairly be said that the imitation of Christ through the imitation of the novice master or mistress was always an essential part of monastic life. Arsenius the Deacon, who had been an imperial tutor in Constantinople before seeking wisdom in the desert, was asked, "'How is it that you with such a good Latin and Greek education ask this peasant about your thoughts?" He replied, "I have indeed been taught Latin and Greek but I do not even know the alphabet of this peasant'" (Ward, 2003, p. xvii).

So too in the Rule of St Benedict (early sixth century), the abbot is likened to Christ. It is instructive that this Rule brings spiritual order into a chaotic world reeling from the collapse of the Western Roman Empire in 476 CE. The language in which it is couched is uncomfortable, even inappropriate today, but the theme of imitation under discipline remains valid: 'The abbot, since he is believed to represent Christ, is to be called "Lord" and "abbot"; not for his own sake, but out of honour and love for Christ' (Dysinger, 1997, p. 149). The flip side of this is that the abbot has to 'behave in such a way as to be worthy of such honour', and Benedict is careful to remind those in authority who they serve, where that authority comes from, and how they are to be judged.

Clearly, a note of caution should be sounded at this point. Such unquestioning obedience is wide open to spiritual abuse, and we must be wary of hierarchical absolutism. From the director's point of view, spiritual arrogance is not very far away, and those directed can easily become inappropriately dependent. What can be distilled from the monastic practice is the important recognition that my humility in listening to my director and following her advice may well serve me in my spiritual journey as the 'voice and will of Christ'. As a director, I need to know that I may well be used by Christ in this way, and prepare accordingly, with due humility, prayerfulness and serious regard to the influence I have.

The ascetic impulse and its tempering

A significant difficulty in using spiritual material from such a distant and alien age lies in the harshness of the disciplines imposed. Benedict doesn't flinch from whipping young monks who get the liturgy wrong. Though self-martyrdom and self-mutilation were quickly discouraged or banned by the Church, the tendency to excess has haunted the practice of Christian discipleship ever since. We find it in the hermits who confined themselves to platforms on pillars, following the fifth-century St Simeon Stylites, through the fifteenth-century flagellants whose self-flogging is still practised in parts of the Iberian Peninsula, to the 'twenty-one to forty days or longer' fasting suggested by Richard Foster in *Celebration of Discipline*. In our own age, it is most evident in spiritual intensity of an unhealthy and often competitive kind. It is worth noting that even the most extreme hermit had a group of people around him or her, supplying food and water and caring for basic needs.

In the face of these extremes of spiritual activity, there is a countervailing tradition of wisdom disseminated by spiritual guides down the ages, of moderation and balance, of reasonableness and boundaried common sense. Its practice can be illustrated from the writings of Orthodox sages guiding people in the use of the Jesus Prayer. From the earliest times, the praying of this classic prayer has been linked with measured breathing. So Gregory Palamas (1296–1357) said that 'slowing down the rhythm of the breathing … helps to hold in check the volatile and easily distracted intellect'. Even he said that this is an exercise for beginners rather than a mechanical end in itself. In the nineteenth century, the Russian Theophan the Recluse warned that 'The various methods described by the Fathers (sitting down, making prostrations, and the other techniques used when performing this prayer) are not suitable for everyone: indeed without a personal director they are actually dangerous.

It is better not to try them.' A century later, Bishop Kallistos Ware comments: 'The utmost discretion is necessary when interfering with instinctive bodily activities such as the drawing of breath or the beating of the heart. Misuse of the physical technique can damage someone's health and disturb his mental equilibrium.'[20]

Two things stand out here. The first is the danger of confusing prayer techniques with the aim and end of prayer, which is union with God by the path of purgation and illumination. The second is the importance of having a spiritual guide to temper our natural tendency to fly before we can walk. In both these senses, the spiritual director offers discipline of a wholesome and gentle kind, a taming, calming influence on the over-exuberant disciple. It is of course a discipline that is invited, accepted, and tested, rather than unthinking subservience to a spiritual guru.

The pastoral theology of Gregory the Great[21]

We have already noted the place of letter-writing in the practice of accompaniment. To this we can now add texts of guidance for directors, in which is implicit the key principle that those who direct need training and supervision as well. The earliest such text is Pope Gregory the Great's *Liber Regulae Pastoralis,* commonly known as *Pastoral Care,* written about 590 CE. It is a primary text for histories of pastoral care and counselling, though at its heart it focuses on the role of the bishop as pastor, spiritual guide, intercessor and disciplinarian, the 'physician of souls'. Of course it raises questions for us in a more professionalized age about differentiation of roles, but its emphasis on oversight, *episcopé,* gives us a theological model for spiritual supervision.

---

20 All three quotes in this paragraph can be found in the excellent articles on Orthodox prayer at www.orthodoxprayer.org/ (accessed 20.11.2018).
21 We have noted a full text of Gregory's work in the bibliography and many editions are available online.

As befits a practical manual, it pays attention to context, to the person being supervised and to the particular spiritual journey so far. Chapter 13 in Book 3, for example, is entitled: 'Those who fear scourges, and therefore live innocently; and those who have grown so hard in iniquity as not to be corrected even by scourges.' It serves as a useful warning against being programmatic in one's approach. Most importantly, though, it points out that those who are imitated and obeyed (in a very hierarchical age) need to be attentive to the wellbeing of their spirits so that, in the words of St Paul, 'after proclaiming to others I myself should not be disqualified' (1 Cor. 9.27). This is summed up helpfully in the brief Book 4. Here Gregory warns against being 'inordinately secure in confidence of strength', glorying in our own reputation and neglecting to put God in the 'place of highest regard'.

The relationship between the director and God exists predictably enough on the prayerfulness of the director. God's part is to remind us of our humanity by bringing our frailty and imperfection into focus: 'Almighty God, though perfecting in great part the minds of rulers, still in some small part leaves them imperfect.' We might say it differently today, reminding ourselves that we are in no way superior to the 'cracked pots' (2 Cor. 4) whom we support, but sometimes the language and style of an earlier age shock us into new insights. God does have a responsibility to remind us of our creatureliness!

Ignatius' *Spiritual Exercises*

Almost a millennium after Gregory, out of the fiery struggles of the sixteenth-century Reformations, emerged the hugely influential figure whom we know as Ignatius of Loyola, founder of the Society of Jesus (Jesuits) and designer of the *Spiritual Exercises*. But first, a confession. I have not felt called to carry out the Exercises myself, though I can see and understand why they are a formative blessing for so many. It makes complete sense to me that Ignatius should write notes for those accompanying others in the business of staying faithful in the turbulent journey of life, but wonder at the wisdom of recreating a monastic environment in which to carry them out. I am also suspicious of any programme that becomes programmatic, a 'one size fits all', though no Jesuit actually suggests that!

The other feature of my confession is an admission that all spiritual directors understand, that a good part of the way we relate to God and the world depends on our personality, our genetic make-up, our training and our environment. It may be that the way I am disposes me to other patterns of spiritual formation, or I may be avoiding something which would be good for me! In any event, my confession reminds me that my limited spiritual experience and map may make me a useful companion to some, and are a reason why others will never seek me out. There are some for whom my guidance would be very unhelpful, and it is important to discern this in accepting (or refusing) an approach.

To return to the subject, Ignatius' Exercises mark a significant change in the history of spiritual direction. Whereas Gregory's *Pastoral Care* was aimed at leaders in a highly structured and boundaried Church, the *Spiritual Exercises* was written for a new breed of outward-looking Christians, peripatetic, busy, moving into unfamiliar spaces where the old rules no longer worked. The style of each reflects this. Gregory writes regulation and wisdom for clearly understood structures. Ignatius outlines a way of living that responds to new uncertainties. 'More than a book, the Exercises are an experience, a great adventure to the heart of God and, therefore, to the real and present needs of the world' (O'Brien, 2011, loc. 164). In the face of the present popularity of the Exercises, often done in groups, it is important to note Ignatius' original intention of one to one guidance, and that they were designed with the Catholic missionary priesthood in view. For an excellent representation of the effect of the Exercises consistently applied over a life-time of spiritual and theological reflection we recommend the reader engage with Gerard Hughes' last book *Cry of Wonder*.

Underlying the difference between Gregory and Ignatius is a key theological issue. Gregory's writing reminds us that Jesus Christ is the same, yesterday, today and forever. God in that sense never changes, and always is. This text focuses on the fixity, the reliability, the unchangeableness of the being and the character of God. Ignatius' writing, on the other hand, points to the fact that we may believe in this reliable God, but we rarely if ever experience life in this way. The journey of human life is riddled with surprises, shocks, unanticipated twists and turns: moving goalposts. At the heart of the Exercises is the insistence that they are notes for travellers, who should never travel alone, but remain close to their Christ and their companion: the director. In the Exercises, God who is always 'real' becomes really real as God comes to life in my life. In spiritual direction, this means that there are twin emphases: the God who is, and the God who becomes, in us.

The Rule of Life

This duality shows up in the idea of the Rule of Life. At the heart of all monastic movements was such a Rule, combining regulations by which the community must live and a set of spiritual principles undergirding those regulations. This twin emphasis on an overarching ethic and the rules that spring from it means that most monastic rules are not neat and tidy, and certainly not legalistic. While every Rule contained detailed instructions, it was at least as important for monks and nuns to have the Rule read chapter by chapter at mealtimes so that its general spirit could be imbibed, inbreathed, inhabited.

In the spiritual direction world, we have grown familiar with the idea of each disciple creating and living by a Rule of Life, and it is often an important focus for director and directee. The monastic origin of the idea of the Rule reminds us that my personal Rule is not individualistic, determining my life alone. Rather it enables me to live well within the community of faithful people. As such, the history of the idea calls us out of our spiritual self-absorption back into the Trinitarian model, that as humans we are created interpersonally, with lives that interpenetrate all other lives under God.

Historically, the monastic rules spilt out of the cloister into a more public space as the monastic ideal began to be reimagined as the *vita apostolica*. From the twelfth century onwards, as Western Europe began to emerge from the turmoil of people movements and invasions and cities developed, clerics began to call 'the ordinary people' to the life which once only monks and nuns could aspire to. The difference of course was that such people could not easily be cloistered, but followed the leader in a much more messy, enthusiastic and sometimes riotous way. Some such movements reinvigorated the monastic movement. We see this in the lives of St Francis and St Clare, for example, for whom the *vita apostolica* was simply a call to Christ-like poverty.

For others, however, much looser associations resulted, and we can illustrate this from the movement we now know as the Beguines, dating back to the eleventh century: groups of lay women in Western Europe who sought to live 'a life of perfection based on praying, sanctified work and mystical pursuit, sometimes with forms of asceticism' (Panciera, 2011, loc. 291). Many of us are now familiar in a tourist environment with the *beguinages* of Belgium, which look for all the world like urban monasteries. In their origins, however, they are much more radical, involving women of all social classes, without formal ecclesiastical supervision, without lifelong vows, simply choosing to live the life of Christ together for a season in disciplined corporate simplicity.

Silvana Panciera describes them romantically in the heading to her Chapter 2 as 'a movement without origins, without a founder, without a common rule, without historiography'. In a technical sense, that is true. What is more important for us is to recognize that they lived 'under the rule of Christ', and knew that they did. There was a shared discipline of values, of behaviours and of practices that enabled them to live the *vita apostolica* in mutual support. To use the language of Kenneth Leech, they were 'soul friends' and no doubt offered one another mutual accompaniment and guidance while pursuing the household arts (notably sewing), works of mercy and the education of poor children. This spiritual networking, as we might call it, enabled them to be faithful to Christ and loyal to one another, obedient but not subservient to an authoritarian and patriarchal church.

The Beguines, then, lived under the rule of Christ without a formally adopted Rule. Their emphasis was on being the body of Christ in the city, acting out Christ's presence towards a suspicious church and a much more welcoming community. It is what in the twentieth century Charles de Foucauld called 'The Life of Nazareth', the informal but structured call of the Little Brothers and Sisters of Jesus who follow him into the urban wastelands.[22]

A new religious landscape

It will not have escaped readers that much of the energy in the regulation and practice of spiritual direction came from the monastic traditions of Christianity, and offshoots from those traditions. In the Christian West, those traditions were brought to an abrupt end in the sixteenth century in areas which became formally Protestant. Even the language of direction changed, and to this day many Protestant Christians avoid using the classical terms out of a presumed desire to avoid a 'Catholic taint'. I even

---

22 See www.jesuscaritas.info.

once had a young student come to me for what he called, 'not spiritual direction'!

But as we noted earlier, the energy for accompaniment predates even the monastic movements. It simply arose from a desire to follow Jesus well, and be helped in following. Though the Protestant and Radical Reformations did not return to the supposed simplicity of the early Church, the dismantling of structures meant that a new wave of spiritual energy generated its own popular and unofficial forms of spiritual accompaniment in the sixteenth and seventeenth centuries. We will now consider two features of that wave: the popularization of devotional writings, and the emergence of radical communities of shared discipleship and discipline.

Popular devotional writing

We have seen how the art of letter-writing, the production of manuals of guidance and books outlining spiritual journeying and ascent formed a central part of the work of direction. One might argue that this was an original purpose for the writing of the various texts of the New Testament.

As the Reformations roughly coincided with the invention of the Western printing press and the expansion of education beyond the monasteries, so writing and reading became the domain of the many rather than the few. The left-wing social historian Christopher Hill observed that: 'Translations of the Bible into English had made it available to new and far wider social groups than hitherto, including artisans and women, and they read their own problems and solutions into the sacred text' (1993, p. 4).

One of the key features of early modern Europe was the inexorable production of devotional texts alongside political ones. This was so much so that by the nineteenth century it is said that there were four books in most households: the

Bible, the Book of Common Prayer, the *Imitation of Christ* by Thomas à Kempis and Bunyan's *Pilgrim's Progress*. Of these we understand three, but the late medieval and very Catholic text by à Kempis is a puzzle until we realize that it too springs from an urbanized, increasingly lay and popular environment in which Christians sought their own way forward rather than by simple obedience to Mother Church.

We can now easily see the negative consequences of such popularization. Not least is what Hill calls 'a biblical culture' in which he describes the Bible irreverently as:

> A huge bran-tub from which anything might be drawn ... The result was disagreement and fragmentation ... Each group of heretics thought they found justification for their positions in the sacred text; nearly all proclaimed the over-riding authority of the Bible. (p. 5)

The positive side of this was that devout Christians (Protestant, Radical and Catholic alike) saw the Bible as a gift, a map for the spiritual life, a map to which all had access. It is no coincidence that the heavily scriptural basis of Ignatius' Exercises was written in the same century. Since the seventeenth century the Bible has been understood much more generally and in a primary way as a key source of spiritual guidance, at the same time as it has slowly lost its use as a text for warmongers and controversialists.

It is important for us to understand the difference between an era of heavy social control, in which the Church sought to determine how people responded to God, and this new, heady age of relative freedom. The element of choice becomes much more strongly a tool of spiritual direction in its own right. Which texts shall I read? How shall I interpret them? Who will help me read them best? As directors, we may take this for granted now, but we need to acknowledge that our power to recommend or censure texts remains intact, and use it with care and discretion.

Furthermore, it is a central pillar of spiritual direction that we allow our directee the freedom of the adult disciple, trust God and make the exercise one of grace, not judgement.

As a postscript on texts, we note that the heyday of popular Christian literature was the nineteenth and twentieth centuries, and spiritual directors need to ask themselves what new textual alternatives are taking their place. In a more transient cultural scene, orality and temporary texts are more likely to dominate, yet the spiritual direction scene remains resolutely embedded in a culture of the written word. The historical antidote to this has been the apophatic tradition or *via negativa*, which approaches God through that which cannot be said about God.

Yet a word-filled approach to God remains equally important. Today's texts of choice come on the mobile phone, in YouTube videos, on social media and in the postmodern poetry of popular music. All these are available to the contemporary disciple of Christ, and this textual space needs to be populated with the wisdom of God and the words of Christian guides. This is for us 'A dramatic challenge to refocus the human senses, not least in its invitation to attend to the Word in the language of everyday' (Gay, 2011, loc. 384).

Communities of shared discipline

The persistence of textuality in Christian spirituality is a testimony to the presence of the eternal Word. The gift of language is a sign of the divine at work in making and remaking us. Similarly, the human hunger for community is a sign of the Holy Trinity in our midst. The Church is the primary sacrament of Christ, a point made in relation to all the sacraments towards the end of Chapter 1.

The turbulent end of the monastic life in much of Europe in the sixteenth century did not put paid to the idea and practice of communities of shared discipline. It simply relocated it, and the character of new groups has much to teach us about the reorientation of the practice of spiritual direction in Protestant circles.

In England, this radical new way of doing community first comes into focus with the Lollards in the fifteenth century, a dispersed movement of people who took their inspiration from John Wycliffe's criticism of the established church and his illegal translation of the Scriptures into English. Refusing to gather under the auspices of the official church, they met in secret places and sought to live a shared life of discipleship less hierarchically, with fewer gender restrictions, abandoning what they thought of as 'priest-craft' and remodelling Christian community in the spirit of Acts 2 read as a communitarian text. Similar experiments popped up all over Europe: the Hussite Christians of Moravia, the Anabaptists of Switzerland and the Netherlands and the Schwenkfelders of Silesia among others.

What was common to them all was the notion that we are not converted to Christ alone, but into a visible community of the saved or the twice-born. Most readers will be familiar with the dangers of such language, but stay with me! These radical Christians described themselves in biblical language as 'Members of the household of God and fellow citizens of the saints, and not of the world' (Yoder, 1973, p. 23). We remain familiar with this language, not least from the liturgical prayers or collects of the Church. But for the Radicals this meant that their primary allegiance was to the bride of Christ, the community to which they were betrothed because they were betrothed to Christ. Their opponents were quick to seize on the less attractive, sometimes destructive versions of this, and Michael Sattler's emphasis on the Christian community as 'our kingdom, fatherland and citizenship' (Yoder, p. 24) is easily lost. In this new citizenship, the mutual support of one's sister and brother Christians leads to physical and spiritual support in all things, admonition where we are going astray, and a united identity in Christ.

The problem with these groups is that they confused the Church Universal or Catholic Church with their little worshipping community, and from this confusion they took centuries to recover. During the seventeenth and eighteenth centuries, however, this radical intensity was tempered by theological pragmatism; others may be Christians too! In this way, the cells of the Lollards and Anabaptists turned gradually into the societies of High Anglicanism and the band-societies of Wesleyan Methodism. We might recognize this today as the remote origin of the house group!

John Wesley said that the purpose of his bands was 'to obey that command of God, "Confess your faults one to another, and pray one for another, that ye may be healed".[23] Before admission, the enquirer is asked a series of questions, notably:

- Do you desire to be told of your faults?
- Do you desire that every one of us should tell you, from time to time, whatsoever is in his heart concerning you?
- Is it your desire and design to be on this, and all other occasions, entirely open, so as to speak everything that is in your heart without exception, without disguise, and without reserve?

After admission, the weekly questions included:

- What known sins have you committed since our last meeting?
- What have you thought, said, or done, of which you doubt whether it be sin or not?

---

[23] The Rules of the Band Societies 1738, drawn up 25 December 1738, in a series of pamphlets printed by J. Paramore in the 1780s, page 1, digitized by Brigham Young University, Utah and available at https://archive.org/details/rulesofbandsocie468wesl (accessed 11/03/2019).

The outcome of this new experimental wave of Christian practice was a commitment to mutual spiritual support that was direct and risky, but thought that the healthy state of the soul of a believer was worth the occasional impertinent question! Of course, such practices were open to abuse, but we must be careful not to read our more sensitive social manners into a rougher age. My grandfather (1891–1982) was a product of this radical small-group shared spiritual discipline, and it kept him faithful through the best part of 50 years as a coal miner, mostly underground.

What are the keys to this spiritual mutuality? In my grandfather's case, the teenage miner who brought him to faith also taught him to crochet, and I detect a strong vein of spiritual friendship which embraced more than just the religious elements of life. Whenever he told that story, there was a deep gratitude that his companion gave him a proper shape for life, and for eternity. Unlike the exclusive emphasis in Aelred of Rievaulx's twelfth-century text *On Spiritual Friendship*, such friendship was neither controlling nor limiting. It was there simply for the asking, and for blessing.

I am also aware, writing this, of how readily my grandfather told such stories, and that story-telling is a key part of spiritual direction. In sharing the narrative of our life within a Christian context, we help weave it into the larger narrative of the story of God, and all we need for this is a willing, wise, often silent and always prayerful listener.

Using the traditions wisely

I began this chapter by stressing that this is not a history of spiritual direction, but simply a selection of episodes which illustrate key emphases and inform our theological reflection. In the course of the chapter I took the risk of expressing some of my own spiritual preferences, and perhaps prejudices! I also warned against using particular traditions as means of spiritual control.

Here it is important for me to stress that I am a director not in the sense of a controller but simply in the twin senses of companion and guide. Rather than forcing those I accompany to 'come home to my tradition with me', noble though that tradition might be, I seek to help others to find and name their own 'home' in the Christian traditions, whether Benedictine, Ignatian, Puritan or Pentecostal, and to explore the riches of that home. Then, from the security of home, I encourage them to continue to explore other traditions through reading and experience, to risk the great adventure that is exhilarating and boundless and takes us way beyond our spiritual comfort zone. And where an old 'home' has become trite or worn, I may also be able to accompany someone into a new 'home', settle them in, and give them the confidence to know that a radical 'rehoming' is not a loss of direction. It is simply a recalibration of our lifelong journey towards union with God.

Reflection and questions

- Might it be a helpful model for us to think of ourselves as 'those who stand in the shadows' like Volmar did for Hildegard? What does this image evoke for you? How might it apply in direction for you?

- Is there any place for the monastic practice of 'discipline under obedience' in today's practice of spiritual direction?

- What spiritual traditions inform your Christian journey and what authority or force do you allow them to have? Do you have a particular 'tradition' in which you pray and retreat? What are the advantages and disadvantages of such positioning?

- What spiritual texts from the traditions inform your journey and your directing/being directed? Are there any texts which you exclude that might challenge or instruct you in less comfortable ways?

8

The Church and Spiritual Direction

As we near the end of our book we turn to locating the practice of spiritual accompaniment within the Church. This raises many questions some of which we will address in this chapter. We begin with thinking theologically about the nature and purpose of the Church and then get into the nitty-gritty of where direction properly sits in her structures, before dealing with local questions about the practice of companionship in local churches.

The Mission of God, the Church and spiritual direction

'I thank you, Father, Lord of heaven and earth, because you have hidden these things from the wise and the intelligent and have revealed them to infants.' So speaks Jesus in Luke 10.21.

God both reveals and hides Godself to us – we noted this through God's presence and absence earlier in the book: with Moses in the unburnt burning bush and in the cloud on the mountain; with Elijah as God passes by and in the following, 'sound of sheer silence'; with the three disciples as Jesus is transfigured before them alongside Moses and Elijah before the cloud hides them once again. In such circumstances the local church gathered week by week is always a miracle. Nowhere else would or could such a mixture of the simple and the learned be assembled as one before the God who mysteriously and often surprisingly calls, gathers, centres and sends God's people. The question this chapter addresses is the relationship between the seeking of God in spiritual direction, especially when that God can be terribly elusive, and the Church both locally and denominationally. We will pick up several ideas and motifs here from the introductory chapter of this book. They bear repeating for emphasis since we think they are some of the unique contributions we are making to a practical theology of spiritual direction.

The Church, theologically, is created and gifted by God. Rowan Williams as Archbishop of Canterbury was often quoted as saying it is the 'pressure of the risen Jesus' that makes the Church happen – and we can read of the first manifestations of this phenomenon in the book of Acts. That is, where people notice the living, risen activity of God in Jesus empowered by the Holy Spirit, there 'Church' will emerge. The Church in the book of Acts is called into being by God, gathers regularly for worship in which it is centred on drinking from the spring of living water, the Holy Spirit, who in turn sends the Church into the world to discover and participate in more of the saving activity of God.

God puts all God's 'eggs' in the Church's basket! Given the human propensity for constantly messing things up this would seem to be a risky business on God's part, but there is no other plan. Between God's revelation and hiding and human heights and depths, that Church happens at all is indeed a miracle. It is therefore worth thinking for a moment about the purpose of the Church. Christians have discussed, argued and fallen out over this question for centuries so we won't solve it finally here. However, for me at least, there is a fundamental tension which gives the Church its energy and life, and that is the tension between what you could call the inward and the outward – or to borrow terms from physics, what is known as centripetal force and centrifugal force.

The Church exists to participate in the eternal worship of God the three-in-one both within and without the actual physical place of worship (I love the counter-intuitive sign above the west door in the chapel at the Queen's Foundation for Ecumenical Theological Education in Birmingham, UK, which reads, as you leave, 'you are now entering a place of worship'). In doing so she joins with all the angels and saints who have gone before and are with us in one communion which cannot be broken. There is within this worship both a centring and a sending. These two acts of God form a polarity which, as we saw in Chapter 1, needs to be held together to create energy and life.

Perhaps you remember that game from childhood where a tennis ball is attached to an elastic rope and the rope is joined to the top of a pole stuck deeply into the ground. Players hit the ball as hard as they can and it swings around for the other player to hit back. To return to the physics of the game – the centripetal and centrifugal forces have to be in equal tension for a good game. If the centripetal force outweighs the centrifugal the ball will simply collapse into the centre post (perhaps it wasn't hit hard or well enough). If the centrifugal force is too great the rope will break and the ball fly off into the distance (unlikely I know but still possible, or maybe the post will leave the ground if it is not anchored strongly enough). When the forces are in equal tension there is a good, fun game and the whole has both a centre (the pole held deeply in the ground) and an edge (the ball whizzing through the air looking for the next impact).

I like this as a picture of the Church because, while it has its limits, both at the centre and the edge the task of us Christians is to participate worshipfully in 'what God is up to.' As we noted in the introduction to this book theologians call this the *missio Dei* – the mission of God, the eternal overflow of love from the heart of God to the world in creation and salvation. God is best thought of therefore as a verb – pure action (as we have seen, the pressure of this action in Jesus through the Holy Spirit creates the Church). The Church at her best participates in this action and is able to form new Christian community around what God is up to at any one time and place in the world. From time to time, however, the centripetal force takes over and the Church dies back (like the collapsing ball) by overly facing inwards. On the other hand we know of movements at the edge of Church that fly off, never to be seen again as they lose their connection to the centre. What is true about the game and the Church is that both are renewed at the edge.[24]

Why have I spent so long discussing this picture of the Church? The reason is that if the task of the Church in our day, arising from the *missio Dei*, is 'to find out what God is doing and join in' (where this God both reveals and hides) and the Church is renewed at the edge, not the centre, then the primary activity before us is the *discernment* of this enigmatic but always active God. And discernment of the movement of God is what happens moment by moment in spiritual direction.

I believe therefore there is an acute connection between the recovery of the charism of spiritual companioning in our day and the future of the Church. There are at least two important reasons for this. First, whether a church (or in fact the Church) lives or dies is above all a *spiritual* question. There is good evidence that local churches with pots of money fade away into nothing just as easily as some poorly resourced churches. It is also true that some rich *and* poor churches flourish. Such churches have recognized that the task is to be centred on God and sent into the world to join in God's work which will be always changing them depending on who and where God sends them to.

Secondly, we can understand local churches as highly complex human entities or 'systems' (we might also say organizations). Let's think about this for a moment; a church

---

[24] There is a lot of historical evidence for the expansion and contraction by dying of the Church and her renewal from the edge or margins – see particularly the work of the missiologist Andrew Walls.

of just 50 people has 1,225 potential one-to-one relationships.[25] Imagine trying to map all those relationships and the potential each of them brings on one piece of paper – almost impossible. This raises the question how change happens in such complex human systems – a moment's reflection shows that it probably isn't in a straight line from point A to point B. That is, as often happens today, for the leaders to put a marker in the imaginary ground at some future date and try to take everyone to that place (as many people in the system will probably resist that imposition). People who study human organizations as systems state that the best way to change them for the better is by finding the key foundational behavioural practices or habits and then focus on introducing those or subtly changing them in a future-oriented direction. The whole system is then slowly 'provoked' into change over time.

Our weather is also a complex system which is very hard to predict (don't we know it!) and doesn't happen in straight lines – you might have heard of the way in which a butterfly flapping its wings in one place can be the cause of a hurricane on the other side of the world. The shape or form of the small eddies in the air caused by the butterfly is exactly the same as the form of a hurricane. As we noted in the introduction of this book this is called a 'fractal' (another word might be microcosm) – another example is what is known as the Romanesco Cauliflower which is pyramid shaped overall as it is in each tiny part of the edible head. Spiritual accompaniment then, I suggest, might just be like the butterfly's wings, causing the Church to rediscover its spiritual DNA over and above the enormous anxieties created by the current long-term decline in attendance and participation. I'm not suggesting for a minute here that we have found the 'silver bullet' to the Church's problems in the Western world. I am noting the fractal connection between the discernment of

---

25 The mathematical formula is $r = [n \times (n-1)]/2$ where r is the number of relationships and n the number of people in a group.

SOUL FRIENDSHIP

God between two people hidden away in a room with the door closed and the discernment of God in the world that the Church can join in. The one practice I suggest can be 'scaled up' from the one-to-one to the many-to-many. There is much more to be said here, but we believe this is one of the unique contributions of this book in connecting spiritual direction with the ability to join in the mission of God.

An example might help us here. For several years now I have been involved in what a group of colleagues call 'deep cultural change' in local churches[26] – facilitating them in this very act of embodying the mission of God in their life together. We have worked with more than a hundred churches now across England and the place that accepted the difficult and often painful changes we were asking them to make the most naturally and easily had a Vicar who had recently trained as a spiritual director and several members who had experienced with her a directed course of prayer and discernment exercises.[27] They have subsequently been on an amazing journey discovering 'people of peace' God has been sending to them in their communities, regularly reading the Bible with these people and taking action for the common good based on what God is up to. They are alive to God in a whole new way.

One further reflection arises from this example. Through this work in congregational change I have come to see how over the last few centuries most local churches have given in to, or been captured by, the culture around us which generally wants to place religion (of whatever kind) in the 'private' sphere of life.[28] I have research data from the churches we have worked

---

26 See www.churchmissionsociety.org/partnership-missional-church (accessed 5.12.18).
27 See www.course2.soulspark.org.uk/ and the associated Grove Book (accessed 7.12.18).
28 There is a longer explanation for how this privatization has come about in my *Forming the Missional Church* (p. 139), or see the more erudite work of Lesslie Newbigin.

with around the country which shows that people in them exhibit fairly high levels of personal, private spirituality and even connections and service in their communities, but the churches they belong to hardly ever act in public in the name of their church, authorized by their governance body, usually the Church Council. When people go out from the church to ask people nearby what they think about what goes on there they often respond, 'What church? I didn't know there was one nearby.'

The Church, however, from its very first creedal statement 'Jesus is Lord' is a public body (sorry, Roman Empire, Caesar isn't as Lordly as you think) – which is why persecution happened to Christians in the first centuries and still does in some places today. And, I suggest, most praying that we do is 'public' prayer – even if we take Jesus' important advice to do it in a room with the door closed (Matt. 6.6). This is because the object of our prayer is God who is King of the coming Kingdom which is always 'at hand' and therefore a public reality (e.g. what happens in the 'town' and 'streets' in Luke 10.1–12 really matters). Or to take a more contemporary example and paraphrasing Thomas Merton: 'Do not go into the desert to escape from people, but to find them in God' (1961, p. 54). Contemplation in this frame *always* leads to public action.[29] Any prayer in the name of the Triune God is also the prayer of the Church which is therefore a public act. And if prayer is a public act, even when practised privately, then I suggest spiritual direction also needs to be understood in this public frame. Remember also the connection we made to *phronesis* as practical wisdom conducted in public earlier in the book. We'll return to this theme below.

Connecting spiritual direction with discernment of God and the task of the Church in joining in with what God is up

---

29 This is exactly the approach of Richard Rohr's 'Centre for Contemplation and Action' at https://cac.org/.

to in this way gives us responses to several further important questions relating to the theme of this chapter which we will now address in turn.

1. Where is spiritual direction and its oversight best placed in the Church?[30]

The answer to this question is very subtle and complex, given the arguments we have heard so far. Perhaps it is best to start with where *not* to place spiritual direction – it should not be at the centre of the Church (by which I mean diocese / denomination), but neither should it be at or beyond the edge of that body! For several years I oversaw the provision of spirituality and spiritual direction in an Anglican Diocese alongside a couple of teams of mixed lay and ordained members. This work sometimes involved watching and engaging with how our neighbouring dioceses placed the same task (readers may know that the 40 or so Church of England dioceses have 40 or so ways of doing everything they do slightly differently!). I watched a diocesan bishop chairing a spirituality group without much success. I also knew the problems that occurred when spirituality and accompaniment were cast adrift to find their own way without connection to the centre (or even a minimal budget to do anything with). I concluded several things reflecting on these experiences.

The first point is that spiritual direction, like God, in many ways needs to be properly hidden and embedded within the organization of the Church. Bishops and senior clergy like Archdeacons do not need to know that much about who is directing, just that it happens – perhaps especially when it is the ordained involved. The task of oversight of the ministry, I came

---

30 I know most about what happens in Anglican Churches in this regard and will share here from my experience – I suspect the principles could be distilled and transferred to other types of Church organization.

to believe, was best located 'at the edge of the centre' and was to create and constantly renew a list of accredited, trained and able accompaniers (more on this subject later) some of whom could be offered to potential directees when a request was received.[31] The actual matching of person to person is always up to God and the individuals involved.

Second, there does need to be a connection to the centre. The bishop (if that is the particular Church's practice) is ultimately the one who holds the oversight of what is offered. Spiritual direction can, I believe, be too hidden as if who is a director and how you find one is some kind of *gnostic* secret code which is virtually impossible to crack. This rather 'old school' approach is breaking down now but still appears from time to time. A good example of an important connection to the centre was when, from a meeting of a few directors discussing themes arising from their ministry (rather than individuals of course) a particular concern was fed gently back to the Bishop and his team for them to hear. This was discernment in action again, I believe.

Proper community and accountability flow from having the provision of spiritual direction placed 'at the edge of the centre'. Being a spiritual accompanier is by its 'hidden' nature a somewhat lonely and isolating ministry. However, if we understand it to be a public ministry in exactly the same way as leading worship is public it is important that there are support and accountability structures in place for it. From time to time spiritual companions might meet together as peers, be offered a learning environment or a quiet day in which to recharge themselves so that they know they are not alone, but part of a wider community of practice. Accountability is also of great importance since the Church doesn't have a great

---

[31] There are important legal reasons for offering choices of director to directees too – since the diocese/oversight body is not responsible for what happens in any particular relationship, only in the provision of accredited people to offer the ministry.

record when allowing two people to be in a room together with the door closed. There is a clear distinction to be made here between hearing confession and spiritual direction since the boundaries around the former are of necessity more formal and prescribed. This is not the place to go into the fine detail of how accountability should happen but questions of training, supervision, safeguarding and insurance[32] need to be addressed fully by the oversight body. We will return to training and supervision below.

2. Is spiritual accompaniment for 'every Christian'?

Having touched on this subject in the previous chapter we address it fully here. The provision of accompaniment for all church members was the urgent and passionate call of Gordon Jeff's *Spiritual Direction for Every Christian*. That it doesn't place a question mark at the end of the title, as I have to this section, is significant. Jeff argues that

> every single Christian would benefit from talking over – even if only once a year – how they were getting on in their Christian pilgrimage, and especially in their direct relationship with God which we call prayer. (2007, p. 6)

He rails, quite rightly, against an elitist view of the calling and ministry of spiritual directors and is clear that there are many more Christian people with the charism for it than has previously been understood.

Nevertheless whenever I hear the word 'every' or 'all' in Church life my idealism antennae flicker into action. I do not believe it is helpful to speak in such terms, not least because I

---

[32] Normally public liability and professional indemnity insurance is required for those who charge a fee for accompaniment. Note the 'public' nature of the ministry once again.

don't think that is how human beings work. In a group of any people faced with a change or new idea there is always a range of responses from 'yes, please!' to 'no, not on your life' with every shade in between. So I would rather start with where we are than where we imagine we might be with an idealized 'everyone'. The 'here and now' is always where God is, not in some imagined ideal future state. I am a realist in that sense. In any case the boundary issues around conducting spiritual direction in a single parish with companions who are also members of the parish are significant and would probably defeat any attempt to bring *everyone* into direction in the way that Jeff imagines.[33]

Rather than saying spiritual companioning is for everyone I would prefer to say that it should be available for *anyone*. That is, when the desire is there within me, when I know the time is now to seek a companion, such a competent person whom God has called and gifted will be there for me when I go asking, seeking and, eventually knocking on their door. As an aside here it is worth remarking I occasionally come across people who say they would like to find a director, but can't seem to match up with the right kind of person or their approach. This is especially the case, I believe for those working at renewing the Church from the edge, as we have noted, in pioneer ministries and Fresh Expressions of Church. Such challenges require further discernment in the wider community of those involved even nationally in spiritual direction and its development. Are our current practices and ways of discerning and developing new companions not adequate for some of the people that may come to us?

In any case making soul friendship available for anyone is an approach that will still require the many more companions

---

[33] There is practice in the Orthodox Church where the task of the clergy is understood to be entirely focused on directing the parishioners in their spiritual life when not presiding at the Liturgy. I am curious as to how this might translate into our Western contemporary contexts, if at all.

that Jeff was so committed to discerning and training but the need for companionship will arise out of desire placed by God in the new directee when the *kairos* time is right. Occasionally I would receive requests from third parties for me to offer some possible companions for their friend or colleague. I always politely refused and waited for the person themselves to make direct contact.

There is another question that Jeff's approach raises and it relates to his last chapter 'Spiritual Direction and Parish Strategy' (pp. 117ff). The use of the word strategy here is interesting as he applies his approach to how to 'organize' parish life. While I don't disagree with much of what he says in the chapter I think there is much more to be said. Reed, Osmer and Smucker (*Spiritual Companioning*) write on the subject of this book from a Protestant perspective in the USA and separate companionship from direction *per se*, developing theology and practice around a wider definition of companionship. Their understanding of companionship is broad and encompasses what we might call 'cell groups' or long-term peer-peer groups for mutual support, challenge and discipleship development. They do have a helpful chapter on congregational life and community drawing particularly on the work of Dietrich Bonhoeffer (2015, pp. 26–50) which resonates with my approach to spiritual direction in congregational life set out here.

To return to the theme of the public / private split which the Church has given in to – following my earlier argument in this chapter – I want to locate spiritual direction as the discernment of God in the public activity of God in the worlds of every member – in their homes, in their communities and in their workplaces. I know from very reliable research that if only 15 per cent or 20 per cent of the people in a human organization adopt a new practice the whole system will eventually come around to a new way of being and behaving. This is what I saw happening in the example I gave earlier. Key people including

THE CHURCH AND SPIRITUAL DIRECTION

the clergyperson adopted a stance of *discernment* aided by some of them being in spiritual direction. This is a realistic approach and one which is entirely achievable over a period of a few years. So we could say spiritual direction is for *every* local church, again as noted in the previous chapter – some people, even many, who are being directed will change the nature of how a church discerns the activity of God and joins in with it over time.

Consequently I do believe every ordained minister should be in spiritual direction.[34] Again there are several reasons for this. The ministerial task (I hesitate to say leadership task first off as that term is so loaded, but that is what it is) is at root a spiritual one as we have seen. We need 'spiritual leaders' because in any human system the leader sets the emotional and spiritual field which everyone else lives and moves within. Such fields can be liberative or toxic or something in between. Where the 'atmosphere' or environment is liberative the local church can be a place where God is discerned, where there is not overly busy activity focused on 'saving' the church and where the people, both newcomers and long-standing members, flourish as the church takes its place in the public life of its community where God dwells, living and active.

If spiritual companionship can be a lonely task, for the ordained leadership it can be doubly so given the lack of a plausibility structure for the role in society (we call this 'role ambiguity'), the pressure to perform from the hierarchy and the people (in different ways, however) and the relentless nature of what confronts the clergyperson daily. All this is set in what is often a competitive atmosphere among colleagues who may also be distant, not just geographically. In my experience of more than fifteen years of working in what is often termed

---

34 This might not be such a difficult task since surveys of Anglican clergy (at least) I have seen and conducted regularly report that around 70%–80% already have a companion relationship with someone.

'clergy development' several things need to be in place for the individual to flourish in such trying circumstances. The number one requirement I would say now is good spiritual companionship. This is because where there is a direction relationship it means that Christian leaders are attending to their spiritual lives in what is a spiritual task. This normally results in the person developing a 'rule of life', a set of commitments, behaviours and practices set in a rhythm of time (daily, weekly, monthly, yearly etc.) which works for them around 80 per cent of the time.[35] Once this is in place what I call a God-centred self-definition is formed in the person who is then able to create and hold the environment in which God's people take up their centring and sent work alongside the Holy Spirit. I have watched joy and true vocational purpose return when this happens.

I also recognize that saying every minister should be in spiritual direction might cut across what I have said earlier about the relationship arising out of a desire for it. There is nothing much worse than a clergy person coming to a first trial session with a new companion and declaring in some form or other (with their arms folded and legs crossed!), 'I'm only here because my last ministry review said I should find someone like you.' Once again overcoming such attitudes can only be by people hearing about the life-giving nature of direction and wanting some of that for themselves. I remember sitting down one day with our diocesan spirituality team and asking ourselves why we were so keen for people to be in direction – what are the 'outcomes' of it if that is an appropriate word here. Amazingly quickly we came up with this list (also referred to in the introduction) which I think is worth reproducing here:

- A listening, loving and discerning heart – with a desire and

---

[35] Once again it is idealistic to think that anyone could obey a rule 100% of the time – I always say 80% is realistic and if we can't make the 80% the rule needs changing on the principle we 'pray as we can, not as we can't'.

willingness to follow Christ.
- Formation of a praying self and living in deeper trust, rooted and grounded in God's love.
- Gradual growth in humility, holiness and the fruit of the Spirit.
- Faith and courage in times of darkness, pain, distress or personal transition.
- Readjustment of the use of time. Less driven or compulsive. Stability.
- Energy for and sustainability of work and ministry – less burnout, self-rejection, failure.
- Affirmation and accountability in relationships with self, God and others.
- Reaching the hidden and darker depths of ourselves in a supportive context.
- Healing – allowing the whole self to be wholly before God and offered wholly to God.
- Ability to make sense of and interpret our experiences of God.
- Those who benefit from accompaniment may discover how best they can accompany others.

3. Are spiritual companions amateurs or professionals?

Margaret Guenther began her book on spiritual direction by stating quite clearly:

> This is a book by an amateur, written for amateurs. 'Amateur' is a word that has been devalued in our time, connoting someone not to be taken seriously, not quite up to snuff, certainly a poor (but usually inexpensive) substitute for the worthy professional. (1992, p. 1)

Guenther goes on to point out immediately that the root of the word amateur is the Latin word to love. An amateur works from and out of love for the task. So immediately the question is set before us; amateur or professional?

Before we delve more deeply it is probably worth pointing out first a comparison to certain sports of yesteryear. Rugby had its amateur and professional codes, cricketers could be divided between the 'gentlemen' (the amateurs) and the players (those who were paid). It is obvious of course that if you were from a certain class with money or, interestingly, had a job in the 'higher professions' you could afford to be an amateur in sports. Others needed to be paid to put food on their family's table. The commercialization of sport in the global economy has changed all that, but the likeness remains. Some people are soul friends because they have other sources of income and often full time jobs, so their direction is 'exercised in the cracks' as Guenther so eloquently puts it (p. 1). Others find the ministry of companionship to be their major work and so begin to charge a fee for their services. Sometimes directors on either side of this divide look rather askance at one another and I wonder why this should be.

There is a further issue to be raised here. If the amateur works out of love, is the professional stuck with sourcing their ministry in the institution, the bureaucracy, 'officialdom'? Certainly in the last fifteen or twenty years in the UK spiritual direction has become more clearly professionalized even if not everyone is paid to direct. When I began working in the area of companionship a single person on the senior diocesan team held 'the list' of directors. No-one else knew how many there were or how many requests came in for a director to said person so we had no idea what the need was for direction or how many we might need to train to meet the need that 'might' be out there! That changed, but it did require some bureaucracy, an agreement around who could be a companion and what spiritual direction was as well as some way of creating a community of practice for those directing others. We made a definitive move from the amateur to the professional, but hopefully not all the way (we never developed a corporate brand and logo for instance!)

By now you might have realized I think the amateur/professional binary or dichotomy is wholly false. What we have here is yet another polarity, an irresolvable tension between the amateur and professional which needs to be held together in creative tension. We do this I believe by understanding being a spiritual director as a *craft*, again as we noted in the Introduction. Interestingly Guenther herself uses the metaphor of the midwife for the task of soul friendship (pp. 82ff) and since midwifery has been around as long as human beings have it is definitely a craft that has its masters, journeywomen and apprentices. We dealt with how to understand spiritual direction as craft in the introductory chapter to this book and it might be worth looking back at that section just now. Any highly skilled craftsperson such as a carpenter or painter begins with a gift (we might say charism) for the craft and a love and desire to practice. They are properly amateur in that sense. However, very quickly – if they are to improve and become skilled – there will be a lot to learn which will require all the domains of learning: cognitive (head knowledge), affective (beliefs, values attitudes) and behavioural (skills and pass-on-able habits and behaviours). It is not surprising that in previous ages guilds arose around particular crafts which were the professional bodies which held the boundaries of the skill, sometimes too tightly of course so that they became 'closed shops'. Nevertheless we can see how the positives and negatives of the amateur/professional polarity play out – and our task is always to accentuate the best of what it is to be amateur *and* professional in spiritual companionship.

4. Are spiritual directors 'born or made'? Can and should they be trained?

The response to our final question then drops out quite easily.

The nature / nurture debate is another false binary since both are required.

My own experience (which as I understand it is not uncommon) was that one or two individuals approached me with the request to be directed. We tested this out for a while and it went along fine (my new directees 'stuck') and so I took on one or two more pilgrims. I then decided it was time to find some 'training'. On the 'training' it was clear that those joining the course were starting at different points (some had not directed anyone as yet but had received a call to explore the possibility of being a director) and while we might refer to what happened as 'training' I have left the word in inverted commas since it was more about discernment than anything else. The question we stayed with was: as I learn about how to be a director in a community of other seekers can we discern together whether this is a gifting I have and want to develop?

It was made absolutely clear that the training was only a beginning. So with the emphasis on discernment and understanding the 'training' as the very beginnings of the craft of being a soul friend we can proceed with caution.

At this point a comparison with a further craft-like skill and profession might be useful. I suspect if you have flown in an aeroplane you would have liked the pilot to have some training! Aircraft pilot training proceeds, I suspect (I'm no expert) first in the classroom, then on a flight simulator, followed by working alongside experienced pilots in the air and eventually 'going solo'. Along the way those with the responsibility will be looking to see if the trainee has the right character and temperament for what might happen – especially in a crisis. The pilots I have known are some of the calmest people when everything is going crazy (unlike me, I'd make a terrible pilot).

The key after all the preparation has to be, however, 'flying hours'. Doing the job and getting the experience under your belt – and talking through any issues that arise with others who know the task. Thus any training course or 'apprenticeship' in spiritual companionship is only as good as the supervision or reflection on practice (*praxis* to use the technical term we introduced at the start of the book) that follows it. I cannot emphasize this enough since in my experience this is where the real learning, growth and development of directors occurs over the long term. It is also the place where the theorists of apprentice-type learning develop the idea of a 'community of practice'. It is where both practical wisdom and technical skill really develop. Given the right approach to supervision by focusing on the director's experience (and not attempting spiritual direction of the absent directee by proxy!) supervision is the number one factor in turning apprentices into 'masters' (forgive the male language) of the craft. And let's remember that people who master a craft usually take years of experiencing all sorts of people, situations and questions in direction, reflecting on that experience with another and applying the learning they develop each time they sit down with another companion. Mastery is slow and deliberate but it does come in God's good time.

Writing this chapter has made me realize once again the central importance that spiritual direction can be to the future of the Church. It sets *discernment* as the core task and grows people with mastery of that craft. It enables the members of local churches, as the skills and insights of discernment diffuse through the congregation, to take up their discipleship as those joining in what God is up to at home, in the wider parish and in their workplaces, if they have them. I wonder what might happen if more resources were made available for finding, developing and setting free our best spiritual directors, just as we invest in the development of our senior clergy. And how the risk and challenge that keeping the ministry suitably 'hidden' in such a circumstance could be met.

Reflection and questions

- Where do you find yourself in relation to the edge and centre of the Church? What does the view look like as you face outwardly or inwardly from where you currently are?

- How helpful is it to understand soul friendship within and alongside the mission of God? What other implications might there be of understanding spiritual direction as a public ministry of the Church?

- Amateur or professional – where are you in this polarity – have you moved around it? You might like to fill in the grid where amateur is on the left and professional on the right of a horizontal line. Above the line are the positives and below the line are the negatives. Fill in the four quadrants thus created and think about what this is teaching you. How can we accentuate the positives of both the amateur and the professional?

- Supervision and a 'community of practice' – if you are a soul friend already, where do you find the place to 'reflect on experience' and move towards mastery of the craft? Do you consider yourself an apprentice, 'journeyman/woman,' or master? How do you pass on what you have learnt to the next generation?

9

Towards a Practical Theology of Spiritual Direction

As we complete this book we reflect on the journey of shared writing and invite the reader to become part of the project (therefore we won't add any extra reflection questions at the end of this chapter). This is an ongoing conversation, with our differences and disagreements reflecting the richness and diversity present in accompaniment. We then summarize our understanding of the content and process of a theology of spiritual direction, offering creative ways of engaging with the material. Finally, we ask whether God might be calling the Church to follow a new, more relational path.

The two authors of this book have disagreed over many things, but we both love the fire metaphor for spiritual direction which features in some way on the cover of this book. The opening chapter draws the picture of a campfire scene where we are attending to three fires, not just one, yet one person is making sure the campfire continues to burn. Somehow, we said, as we attend to the fire of God burning in the room outside us, this also kindles the fires burning within our own hearts.

The process of writing this book has been a little like sitting around that campfire, attending to God's fire burning in our hearts as we have talked, wrestled and refined our thoughts. Our conversation has been a three-way dialogue, but as we wrote we became aware that we were drawing you, the reader, into this unfinished conversation. This is a practical theology, which asks the questions 'How then do we live?' and 'How then do we accompany others?' If it helps you to explore those questions and come up with even more creative practice, we shall be content. If, on the other hand, it simply turns into another book of theological theory, an interesting conversation that alters nothing, we should be deeply disappointed.

In a way, our journey of writing together has taught us something about the process of spiritual direction and helped us in our task of theological reflection on our practice. Neither of us could have written this book alone, and our interaction has reminded us that Jesus sent the disciples out in pairs (Luke 10.1). Solitary ministry is a heresy, and a team of three tends towards a committee! The one-to-one of writing together and of sharing in the journey of spiritual direction are both reminders that we guide and are guided much as Jesus and his disciples were. The academic discipline of theology can be a deeply competitive and quarrelsome one, and we hope that we have modelled something a little different in committing ourselves to this short journey of writing.

Then too, the space and difference between us provided a centre outside us in which the other has confirmed or challenged the things we have written, as iron sharpens iron. Genuine differences between us generated energy and life for the project. We have not agreed on everything, and each of us would have written the other's chapters differently. What we have had to do, however, is to own every chapter as coming from both of us. The Christian tradition has always been one of shared obedience to the whole gospel, even the parts or actors we find it difficult to agree with. This models for us the differences, diversity or even disagreements between director and directee, in which we are reminded that they don't necessarily need to share the same theological position to have a creative and fruitful relationship.

And in that external centre space in which we have wrestled, the Spirit of God has been able to move and contribute creatively. We must be careful here and not claim inspired status for what is, after all, only a book written by two 'white, male, Anglican priests firmly in the second half of life'. But of course God is part of this enterprise, and we trust that we have heard the voice of God just as we trust that we hear it in the to and fro of spiritual direction.

We have listened in particular ways too. As spiritual directors, it would be strange if we weren't attentive to each other's voices, unspoken prompts, body language, and partially told stories. We have been tempted to project our own insights onto what we have heard from the other, and we have cautioned ourselves not to read our personal experience into the life story of the one we were listening to. It's sometimes been hard to receive challenging words, and learning this humility is part of the process of spiritual accompaniment, both ways.

And we are unique individuals with a shared story. Over the years, we have been variously teacher and student, fellow mission partners, and now colleagues in a specific ministry. The Christian Church is a small pond, and many of us know people in a range of roles. We have needed to learn a new way of relating that was appropriate to this task, professionally boundaried but not excluding the possibility of friendship as well. This tension too is well known in the world of spiritual direction, as Aelred of Rievaulx reminded his Cistercian monks in Wensleydale in the twelfth century in *Spiritual Friendship*. In the monastery, there is a formal hierarchy of obedience. At the same time, between those who obey and are obeyed, there will emerge friendships. Those friends are:

> The partner of your soul, to whose spirit you join and link your own and so unite yourself as to wish to become one from two, to whom you commit yourself as to another self, from whom you conceal nothing, from whom you fear nothing. (Aelred, 2010, p. 89)

Because of this and the creative dynamic between us we have called this text *Soul Friendship*, and in the book as a whole it would be misleading to call this final chapter a 'conclusion' to our practical theology, a locking down of the facts and truths and insights contained within, as that word originally meant. Conversations don't really have conclusions. They have episodes, pauses, suspensions, but the unfinished conversation will be picked up again one day. Each time a new reader picks the book up, the conversation grows and the story continues. In writing, we have simply aimed to contribute to the great conversation with the God who draws near to us all and draws us nearer to each other. Here too we find echoes of the great spiritual task of repentance (purgation, challenge), illumination (learning and insight) and union.

Another aspect of the unfinished nature of the book lies in the voices that have not been heard, which are manifold. It is a worthwhile question for you to ask how you would have set about this task, and which voices (apart from your own) you have missed hearing. I will never forget the person who came to me once and told me how much she appreciated my preaching. Before I had the chance to swell with pride, she continued, 'But there's one small problem. You always assume that "normal" means "married", and I'm not married. All your examples presume that "married" equals "normal", and that makes it hard for me to hear what you are saying.' Have we, the authors, missed something as fundamental as this in our writing? In any event, we would love to hear your voice, and this is a real invitation to write to us and keep the conversation going!

Towards a practical theology of spiritual direction

One of the clichés beloved of those who teach others to preach is, 'Say what you're going to say, then say it, then say what you've said.' I'm not sure what I think about the half-truths enshrined in it and am certainly not about to plough through a précis of each chapter again. But it may be helpful, having said something about our experience of writing and what that teaches us about direction, to look at the theological flow of the book as a whole.

The first observation is that, unusually for a practical theology work, we have used some of the categories of systematic theology as the organizing structure. Why? Partly because it makes a slightly polemical point. Practical theology is sometimes regarded as the 'soft' cousin of theoretical, 'more academic' theologies, whether systematic, historical-critical or any other. Structuring our book in this way enables us to challenge this assumption, and to say more positively that practical theologians are interested in the same issues as theoretical theologians, even though we approach them from different methodologies and perspectives. We have also wondered whether our arrangement of the chapters is the right one (introduction, God, people, Jesus etc.), moving in and out of the 'above' and 'below' which is why in the Introduction we suggested that you, the reader, take responsibility for choosing the starting point! Apply through *praxis* what we have written to your own context, needs and insights.

The second, and linked, observation is that theology is the servant of the Church, and the structure we have used draws attention to the key foci in the life of the Christian community. To do theology from any Christian perspective is to adhere to a long and consistent obedience to God, our relationship with God, and ultimately God's will. So for example, you cannot do 'good' theology without engaging rigorously with the complex of ideas around salvation, as we do in Chapter 4.

What then is the flow of this book? If we use another metaphor, that of a drama, we can describe the first two chapters as presenting the *dramatis personae,* the characters in the play. Many of us remember from GCSE or A Level days the agony of trying to master the lengthy lists in Shakespeare's plays. Unlike this, our theological *dramatis personae* is simple: you, me, us, them, God, and always in relation to God. That's why we put God first!

Then of course the action begins, and we remember one of the threads that run through this book: 'God is a verb, not a noun.' That action has two facets, the constant drawing near of God, and the transformative impact of that drawing near on each individual and on the human community. This action is unpacked in the third and fourth chapters.

The second quartet of chapters deals with the modes of engagement between us and God: the Holy Spirit, the Holy Scriptures, the Holy Church and (dare one capitalize it!) the Holy Tradition. If that makes you bristle, bear in mind that it is slightly tongue in cheek, but it is important for us to understand in this theological journey that engagement with God is by definition 'holy', and all those modes by which we are able to meet God (and God us) partake of the holy character of God. These are our sources of revelation, and of course they have been a hotbed of controversy down the ages. Where does the priority lie? Which sources are 'sound' and which are liable to 'deceive'? Theologians will for ever pontificate about this, while the humbler sort recognize that the divine - human conversation is not constrained or contained by theological rules.

Of course, this means that you could have started the book at any point and wheeled from there around the other chapters. Some of you have skipped straight to this conclusion anyway, so you are invited to choose your starting point. Let the book fit your journey, not force you onto its own trajectory. If you have ploughed through the whole book already, it may be that now is the time to revisit specific sections to wrestle with them more fully. To reiterate, conversations don't have conclusions, and this text is for us much more like a conversation than a book.

In short, we have held two theological traditions in tension, one more cyclical (practical theology) and one more linear (systematics), reinforcing the idea of dialogue between the academic and the everyday, the intellectual and the earthed. You may also have noticed a further polarity, between institutional loyalty and doctrinal boundedness on the one hand, and an ecumenical approach which regularly crosses or challenges that loyalty and our often rigid theological boundaries. Our theology of spiritual direction describes a journey of risk-taking, a process of becoming which leads through purgation and illumination to the final promise of union with God. This process can be centred in our own traditions and be radically open ecumenically to others. In this we hope our theology is also an 'ecumenical theology of spiritual direction'.

Spiritual direction as discernment in community

Throughout the book, we have emphasized the fact that to be human is to be in community, reflecting the three-in-oneness of God. The consequence is that spiritual direction is not just for individuals but is the task of communities – of churches – too. Walter Wink used the letters to the churches in Revelation 2-3 to talk about the 'deep character' of each of those churches in Asia Minor, the 'angels of the churches' as John writes (1986, pp. 69ff). As we noted in the previous chapter, local churches are always little 'miracles'. Where else in society would such a collection of people kneel together as one body? Just as individuals have personalities, character traits, leanings and tendencies, so too Christian communities have personalities and characters which are deeply embedded in their stories, and not entirely dependent on the particular individuals who are currently part of that community.

So, important as it may be to ask what 'purpose-driven church' (Rick Warren), and 'authentic Christian leadership' (Aubrey Malphurs) might mean for our congregation, for us the central issue has to be enabling church communities to *encounter* and wrestle with God, *discern* the voice of God, *live* as 'little bodies of Christ' enacting the Kingdom of God. Alongside our ministry of spiritual direction, both of us have over the years engaged with congregations in this way, facilitating the conversion of communities through repentance, illumination and ultimately union with God. It may be a zany dream, but we wonder what it would look like if a congregation invited someone to be its spiritual director? Various models of 'mission accompaniment' are available and have been experimented with in recent decades. We think there is much more work to be done on the 'scalability' of spiritual direction to a whole congregation. Is it one person or a team who could sit together with people becoming 'detectives of divinity'? Where are the appropriate boundaries in such an enterprise? How are those in whom God is at work, but are not yet part of the worshipping community, to be appropriately involved?

On the way down this road towards corporate spiritual direction, we need to raise the profile of accompaniment, to preach and teach its availability and its significance, while training a new generation of directors whose focus will be on the 'ordinary folks of the kingdom'. To this end, we will need to identify those being called into this ministry with a much broader range of personalities, skills sets and life experiences. It is no secret that the clergy (a dominant group as spiritual directors) cluster around a rather narrow and unrepresentative group of personality types, and unsurprisingly, contemplatives are drawn to this vocation more often than activists. The underlying assumption that quieter, reflective, often introverted people are a better fit in this ministry needs challenging, both in the mind of the Church and among those who encourage these vocations. The reader could refer back here to what we said about the use of psychological personality profiling in Chapter 2.

In this, there is a challenge for the establishment, the senior leadership of denominations. I still remember a former bishop of Exeter in the 1980s making 'mission, not maintenance' his strap line, and at the time it was exciting to hear a bishop speak like that. The dynamic message that the Church could not complacently go on doing things the way it had for hundreds of years, with a centripetal and parochial approach to its ministry, cohered with the catastrophic decline in church attendance in the half-century after the Second World War.

The danger in that was that we tended to respond with programmatic approaches. 'If only', we said, 'we changed our music, or our training, or our vision statements, or even our theology, the church would begin to flourish.' The solution was in our hands, and we instituted many good things: a Decade of Evangelism, Mission-Shaped Church, Pioneer ministries and Fresh Expressions among them. For Anglicans in England, the most recent programmatic move is that of Resource Churches. Of course there was fruit; there always is. All the time, though, there was a quiet voice in the background asking us for God's opinion and the eternal question: 'What's God up to here?' One of the questions that we ought to be asking is whether God might not have a hand in the decline, seeking to move us in an entirely new direction.

The mission of God and spiritual direction

Many of you reading this will already be thinking as we have discussed already, 'Ah! *Missio Dei*. Mission is the work of God in which we participate.' You might have ploughed through the seminal tome *Transforming Mission* by the South African missiologist David Bosch, so tragically killed in a car accident in 1992. In the very short section of Chapter 12 that deals with Mission as *Missio Dei*, Bosch said:

> Mission is not primarily an activity of the church, but an attribute of God. God is a missionary God ... To participate

in mission is to participate in the movement of God's love towards people, since God is a fountain of sending love. (1991, p. 390)

It is precisely that participation in the 'movement of God's love' about which we have written in this book, and we are persuaded that spiritual direction is at the heart of Christian mission, because it helps Christian disciples to recognize the movement of love, to respond to it both in relation to God and to God's world. Bosch's last words in this book, with the phrase 'spiritual direction' substituted for the word 'mission', reads like this:

Spiritual direction is, quite simply, the participation of Christians in the liberating mission of Jesus, wagering on a future that verifiable experience seems to belie. It is the good news of God's love, incarnated in the witness of a community, for the sake of the world. (p. 519)

A challenge to spiritual anxiety

We dare to believe too that putting spiritual accompaniment at the heart of the life of the Church might also be an antidote to the gloom that hangs over wide areas of the institutional Church, and it's not unrelated to a rediscovery of the organic link between mission and spirituality. Both of us accompany Christian leaders in our work of direction, and are struck by the weight of responsibility, the burden of expectation and the sense that much in the Church is 'falling apart'. When this is coupled with performance targets and a strong sense of obligation and duty, it is not difficult for a Christian minister to turn this gloom into a sense of personal failure and letting God down. At this point, it becomes difficult to accept the idea of graced love, about which we have written extensively throughout. Our spiritual health is instead measured by success and our usefulness to the Kingdom of God.

If we are not entirely demoralized or exhausted by now, we try to carry the burden of atonement for the failures and sins of the Church, losing sight of the redemptive impact of the gospel. It is not, of course, our responsibility as directors to tell people 'well done' for the sake of it, to delude or to suggest that all is well when it is patently not well. But it is at least part of our endeavour to introduce people to God as God is and not to God as imagined and constructed in their lives and ministries. Perhaps the greatest temptation to idolatry in the contemporary Church is the assumption that I or we can save it from its ultimate demise. This redeemer mentality will destroy us, and it will not fix the Church.

Where next?

Throughout this book, we have worked on the theological assumption that God is active in the world, constantly drawing near. Spiritual accompaniment is a way of discerning that activity, and of engaging with it creatively, as individuals and as congregations of the faithful. Because this is so, it is our responsibility as Christian disciples to seek that discernment and engagement, and our task as church leaders and spiritual directors to encourage it. Where churches have become locked in routine and unthinking religious practice, we have a prophetic responsibility to challenge the Church, calling it to reset its priority back to a dynamic and creative relationship with God. To echo the last words of Kenneth Leech in *Soul Friend*, each of us is called to be a guide who 'Points always beyond herself to the Kingdom and the Glory' (1994, p. 188). Our prayer for ourselves and our readers is that everything that hinders that work will be stripped away, and that the Church will be restored to the simplicity of the gospel: the eternal love of God revealed in Jesus Christ.

Bibliography

Kindle texts are paginated variously. Where they are indexed by page number that is indicated in the text as (Taylor, p. 280). Where they are indexed by Kindle Location that is indicated as (Taylor, loc. 280).

OED = Oxford English Dictionary (online edition)

Bibele e Halalelang, 1909 rev. 1987, Cape Town: Mokgatlo wa Bibele wa Afrika e Borwa.

A. C. Spearing, ed. and trs., 2001, *The Cloud of Unknowing and Other Works*, London: Penguin.

Aelred of Rievaulx, 2010, *Spiritual Friendship*, Collegeville: Liturgical Press.

Joseph Baird, 2006, *The Personal Correspondence of Hildegard of Bingen*, Oxford: Oxford University Press.

Paul Ballard and Stephen R. Holmes, eds, 2005, *The Bible in Pastoral Practice: Readings in the Place and Function of Scripture in the Church*, London: Darton, Longman & Todd.

William Barry, 2004, *Spiritual Direction and the Encounter with God: A Theological Inquiry*, rev. edn, Mahwah: Paulist Press.

William Barry and William Connolly, 1986, *The Practice of Spiritual Direction*, New York: HarperCollins.

Stephen B. Bevans and Roger P. Schroeder, 2011, *Prophetic Dialogue: Reflections of Christian Mission Today*, Maryknoll: Orbis.

David Bosch, 1991, *Transforming Mission: Paradigm Shifts in the Theology of Mission*, Maryknoll: Orbis.

BIBLIOGRAPHY

Anne Brennan and Janice Brewi, 1985, *Mid-Life Directions: Praying and Playing Sources of New Dynamism*, Mahwah: Paulist Press.

Christopher Bryant, 1983, *Jung and the Christian Way*, London: Darton, Longman & Todd.

Eileen Burke-Sullivan and Kevin Burke, 2009, *The Ignatian Tradition (Spirituality In History)*, Collegeville: Liturgical Press.

Helen Cameron, Deborah Bhatti, Catherine Duce, James Sweeney, Clare Watkins, 2010, *Talking about God in Practice: Theological Action Research and Practical Theology*, London: SCM Press.

Mihaly Csikszentmihalyi, 1998, *Finding Flow: The Psychology of Engagement with Everyday Life*, New York: Basic Books.

Sarah Coakley, 2013, *God, Sexuality and the Self: An Essay on the Trinity*, Cambridge: Cambridge University Press.

Joanna Collicutt, 2015, *The Psychology of Christian Character Formation*, London: SCM Press.

Oliver Davies, ed., 1989, *The Rhineland Mystics: An Anthology*, London: SPCK.

Doctrine Commission of the Church of England, 1987, *We Believe in God*, London: Church House Publishing.

Luke Dysinger, tr., 1997, *The Rule of Saint Benedict Latin and English*, Santa Ana: Source Books.

Umberto Eco, 1986, *Art and Beauty in the Middle Ages*, Yale: Yale University Press.

Umberto Eco, 2002, *On Beauty: A History of a Western Idea*, London: Secker & Warburg.

Rosy Fairhurst, 2012, *Uncovering Sin: A Gateway to Healing and Calling*, London: SPCK.

Richard Foster, 1978, *Celebration of Discipline*, London: Hodder & Stoughton.

James W. Fowler, 1981, *Stages of Faith: The Psychology of Human Development and the Quest for Meaning*, San Francisco: Harper and Row.

Doug Gay, 2011, *Remixing the Church: Towards an Emerging Ecclesiology*, London: SCM Press.

Elaine Graham, Heather Walton and Frances Ward, 2005, *Theological Reflection: Methods*, London: SCM Press.

Gregory the Great, 1950, *The Book of the Pastoral Rule*, Ancient Christian Writers Vol. 11, Mahwah: Paulist Press.

Pete Greig, 2007, *God on Mute: Engaging the Silence of Unanswered Prayer*, Eastbourne: Survivor.

Stanley J. Grenz, 2001, *The Social God and the Relational Self: A Trinitarian Theology of the* Imago Dei, Louisville: Westminster John Knox.

Margaret Guenther, 1992, *Holy Listening: The Art of Spiritual Direction*, London: Darton, Longman & Todd.

Malcolm Guite, 2012, *Sounding the Seasons: Seventy Sonnets for the Christian Year*, Norwich: Canterbury Press.

Christopher Hill, 1993, *The English Bible and the Seventeenth-Century Revolution*, London: Allen Lane.

Liz Hoare, 2015, *Using the Bible in Spiritual Direction*, London: SPCK.

Richard Hooker, 1907, *Of the Laws of Ecclesiastical Polity*, 2 Vols, London: Dent.

Gerard Manley Hopkins, [1953] 1986, *Gerald Manley Hopkins: Poems and Prose*, London: Penguin.

Gerard W. Hughes, 2014, *Cry of Wonder: Our Own Real Identity*, London: Bloomsbury.

Gordon Jeff, 2007, *Spiritual Direction for Every Christian*, London: SPCK.

Tim Keller, 2008, *The Reason for God*, London: Hodder & Stoughton.

David H. Kelsey, 2009, *Eccentric Existence: A Theological Anthropology*, 2 Vols, Louisville: Westminster John Knox.

Kenneth Kirk, 1931, *The Vision of God: The Christian Doctrine of the Summum Bonum*, London: Longmans, Green & Co.

James Henry Owino Kombo, 2016, *Theological Models of the*

Doctrine of the Trinity: The Trinity, Diversity, and Theological Hermeneutics, Carlisle: Langham Global Partnership.

Kenneth Leech [1977], 1994, *Soul Friend: Spiritual Direction in the Modern World*, new revised edn, London: Darton, Longman & Todd.

Aubrey Malphurs, 2013, *Advanced Strategic Planning: A 21st Century Model for Church and Ministry Leaders*, Grand Rapids: Baker.

Thomas Merton, 1961, *New Seeds of Contemplation*, Boston: Shambhala.

John Milton, 1990, *Complete English Poems, Of Education, Areopagitica*, Dent: London.

Virginia Mollenkott, 1994, *The Divine Feminine: The Biblical Imagery of God as Female*, New York: Crossroad.

Jürgen Moltmann, 1974, *The Crucified God*, London: SCM Press.

Francesca Aran Murphy, 1995, *Christ the Form of Beauty: A Study in Theology and Literature*, Edinburgh: T&T Clark.

Henri Nouwen, 1994, *The Return of the Prodigal Son: A Story of Homecoming*, London: Darton, Longman & Todd.

Kevin O'Brien SJ, 2011, *The Ignatian Adventure: Experiencing the Spiritual Exercises of St. Ignatius in Daily Life*, Chicago: Loyola Press.

Gordon Oliver, 2006, *Holy Bible, Human Bible: Questions Pastoral Practice Must Ask*, London: Darton, Longman & Todd.

Rudolf Otto, tr. John W. Harvey, 1958, *The Idea of the Holy*, 2nd edn, Oxford: Oxford University Press.

Silvana Panciera, tr. Piero Giorgi, 2011, *The Beguines: Women in Search of Sanctity within Freedom*, Independent publication.

Jaroslav Pelikan, 1984, *The Vindication of Tradition: 1983 Jefferson Lecture in the Humanities*, Yale University Press.

Ann Persson, 2010, *The Circle of Love: Praying with Rublev's Icon of the Trinity*, Abingdon: Bible Reading Fellowship.

Eugene Peterson, 2005, *Christ Plays in Ten Thousand Places*,

London: Hodder & Stoughton.

Sue Pickering, 2008, *Spiritual Direction: A Practical Introduction*, Norwich: Canterbury Press.

Angela H. Reed, Richard R. Osmer and Marcus G. Smucker, 2015, *Spiritual Companioning: A Guide to Protestant Theology and Practice*, Grand Rapids: Baker Academic.

William Reiser, 2004, *Seeking God in All Things: Theology and Spiritual Direction*, Collegeville: Liturgical Press.

Richard Rohr, 2012, *Falling Upward: A Spirituality for the Two Halves of Life*, London: SPCK.

Hans Rookmaaker [1978], 2010, *Art Needs No Justification*, Vancouver: Regent College Publishing.

Nigel Rooms, 2011, *The Faith of the English: Integrating Christ and Culture*, London: SPCK.

Nigel Rooms, 2012, 'Paul as Practical Theologian: *Phronesis* in Philippians', *Practical Theology*, Vol. 5.1, pp. 81–94.

Nigel Rooms, 2014, *Forming the Missional Church*, Cambridge: Grove.

Edward Schillebeecx, 1987, *Christ the Sacrament of the Encounter with God*, Franklin, Wisconsin: Sheed & Ward.

Peter Senge, C. Otto Scharmer, Joseph Jaworski, and Betty Sue Flowers, 2005, *Presence: Exploring Profound Change in People, Organizations and Society*, London: Nicholas Brealey.

Philip Sheldrake, 2001, *Befriending our Desires*, London: Darton, Longman & Todd.

Charles Sherlock, 1991, *God on the Inside: Trinitarian Spirituality*, Canberra: Acorn Press.

John V. Taylor, 2004, *The Go-Between God: The Holy Spirit and the Christian Mission*, London: SCM Press.

Adrian Thatcher, 2011, *God, Sex and Gender: An Introduction*, Chichester: Wiley-Blackwell.

R. S. Thomas, 1993, *Collected Poems 1945-1990*, Phoenix.

Martin Thornton, 1984, *Spiritual Direction: A Practical Introduction*, London: SPCK.

BIBLIOGRAPHY

Angela Tilby, 2009, *The Seven Deadly Sins: Their Origin in the Spiritual Teaching of Evagrius the Hermit*, London: SPCK.

Stephen Torr, 2013, *A Dramatic Pentecostal/ Charismatic Anti-Theodicy Improvising on a Divine Performance of Lament*, Eugene: Pickwick Publications.

H. E. W. Turner, 1952, *The Patristic Doctrine of Redemption: A Study of the Development of Doctrine During the First Five Centuries*, Eugene: Wipf & Stock.

Ann and Barry Ulanov, 1982, *Primary Speech: A Psychology of Prayer*, Louisville: Westminster John Knox.

Benedicta Ward, tr., 2003, *The Desert Fathers: Sayings of the Early Christian Monks*, London: Penguin Classics.

Rick Warren, 2002, *The Purpose Driven Life*, Grand Rapids: Zondervan.

Samuel Wells, 2004, *Improvisation: The Drama of Christian Ethics*, London: SPCK.

Samuel Wells, 2015, *A Nazareth Manifesto: Being with God*, Oxford: Wiley Blackwell.

James Whitehead and Evelyn Eaton Whitehead, 1980, *Method in Ministry: Theological Reflection and Christian Ministry*, New York: Harper & Row.

Walter Wink, 1986, *Naming the Powers: The Invisible Forces that Determine Human Existence*, Philadelphia: Fortress Press.

John H. Yoder, ed. and tr., 1973, *The Legacy of Michael Sattler*, Scottdale: Herald Press.

Frances Young, 2011, *God's Presence: A Contemporary Recapitulation of Early Christianity*, Cambridge: Cambridge University Press.

William Young, 2007, *The Shack*, London: Hodder & Stoughton.

John D. Zizioulas, [1985], 2004, *Being as Communion: Studies in Personhood and the Church*, London: Darton, Longman & Todd.

John D. Zizioulas, 2010, *The One and the Many: Studies on*

God, Man, the Church, and the World Today, Alhambra, CA: Sebastian Press.

Index of Names and Subjects

39 Articles 123

á Kempis, Thomas, *The Imitation of Christ* 150
accompaniment *see* spiritual direction
accountability 165–6
addiction, as disordered desire 47–8
Aelred of Rievaulx 154, 179
amateurs, directors as 171–3, 176
Anabaptists 152, 153
anthropology:
 cultural 72–3
 theological 42–60
anxiety, spiritual 186–7
apophatic tradition 39, 48, 110, 151
Aristotle, and knowledge 9–11
Arsenius the Deacon 141
asceticism 5, 53, 140, 142–3, 147
atonement 81–4, 86, 87
attunement 113–14, 117
Augustine of Hippo 111
authority of scripture 122–5, 136, 150

Ballard, Paul and Holmes, Stephen 120
baptism:
 as drama 135
 as encounter with God 34
 in the Spirit 99–100, 108–9
 and *theosis* 71, 72, 96–7
Barry, William SJ 3, 8–9
Basil of Caesarea 36 n.6
Beguines 147–8
being-in-communion:
 God as 69
 humans as 43–5, 46, 50–1, 52, 56, 59
 Jesus as 68
Bell, John 23
Benedict of Nursia 141, 142
Bernard of Clairvaux 95–6, 137–8
Bevans, Steve and Schroeder, Roger 24
Bible *see* scripture
bishops, and oversight of spiritual direction 165
body:
 in direction 51–2, 59
 and incarnation 17, 62–4, 66–7, 68–70, 82
 and somatic empathy 65–6

Bonhoeffer, Dietrich 168
Bosch, David 185–6
boundaries of spiritual direction 59, 67–8, 75, 121, 167
Bunyan, John, *Pilgrim's Progress* 150

Cappadocian Fathers 36
Carter, Sydney 23
cell groups 116, 168
charismatic tradition 99–100, 107, 129
Christ 'Pantocrator' icon 64, 69, 76
Christ-hymn, in Philippians 61–2, 72
Christendom, end 14–15
Church:
  as context for spiritual direction 164–6
  as gift 158
  and mission 14–15, 33, 159–60, 162, 185–6
  purpose 158–9
  as sacrament 151
  and sacraments 33–5
  and spiritual direction 157–76, 183–5
  and State 14–15
Clare of Assisi 147
Clement of Alexandria 92–3
clergy, need for spiritual direction 169–70
The Cloud of Unknowing 11, 49, 91–2
Coakley, Sarah 48–9, 53, 102–3
Collicutt, Joanna 57–8
community:
  and individual 43–5, 183–5
  and shared discipline 151–4
companionship 6, 7, 9, 168
  and Holy Spirit 99–118
  see also spiritual direction
confession:
  and purgation 89–90
  and spiritual direction 166
Connolly, William 3
consolations 115
contemplation 48–9, 53, 95, 129, 163
conversation, prayer as 37–40
correlation, and use of scripture 130–32, 133 n.18
counselling, and spiritual direction 12, 58, 75
craft 10–11, 13, 16, 18, 173, 174, 176
creation:
  in image of God 16, 30, 43–5, 46–7, 52, 60, 71, 103
  redemption 70
creativity:
  of God 25, 27, 30
  and inspiration 103–6, 125
  spiritual direction as 13, 18, 132
Csikszentmihalyi, Mihaly 75 n.12

dance, divine 23–7, 31
de la Mare, Walter 19–20
Descartes, René 43
desert Fathers and Mothers 7, 47–8, 140–41
desire, disordered 46–9, 50, 78
desolation 8, 74, 83–5, 115
despair 82–3, 112
devotion, popular texts 149–51
directors:
  as amateurs/professionals 171–3, 176
  guidance texts 143–4
  hiddenness 138
  supervision 53, 58, 67–8, 120, 143, 164–5, 175, 176
  training 173–5, 184
discernment:
  of God 160, 161–2, 163–4, 168–9, 183–4
  and recognition 115
  and scripture 123
  in spiritual direction 15, 32, 90, 106–8, 167, 174–5, 187
Docetism 68
Donne, John 42, 43

empathy 65–6
encounter with God 9, 20–21, 26, 27–8, 32, 33, 40
  and Holy Spirit 101–2
  in sacraments 33–5, 40
  through scripture 30–33, 40, 128–9
Enlightenment 11, 14, 82
Enneagram 55
Erikson, Erik 57
essence of God 35–6, 38, 95
Evagrius Ponticus 4, 7, 48
evil 39, 40–41, 79, 82–3
experience, personal, and scripture 130–32

Fairhurst, Rosy 59
flow 75 n.12
Foster, Richard 142
Foucauld, Charles de 148
Fowler, James 57
fractals 16, 18, 27, 161–2
Francis of Assisi 147
Freud, Sigmund 55, 114

Gandhi, Mohandas K. 50
Gay, Doug 151
gender 52–3, 68–9
  and direction 5
  and God 28
  and language 36–7, 102–3, 117–18
generosity of God 27
gift:
  Church as 158
  creativity as 30
  God as 45, 47, 49, 82, 85–6
  grace as 78, 86, 88, 96, 106
  liberation as 51
  salvation as 78, 82–6
  spiritual 106–8

gifts:
  of the Holy Spirit 106–8, 109–110
  personal 117
glossolalia 100, 109–110
Gnosticism 68, 165
God:
  beauty of 28–30
  encounter with 9, 20–21, 26, 27–8, 32, 33, 40
  as gift 45, 47, 49, 82
  and *missio dei* 15, 33, 159–60, 162, 176, 185–6
  as mother and father 28
  and spiritual direction 19–42, 62
  as Trinity *see* Trinity
  as verb 3, 22–3, 36, 40, 159, 182
  see also immanence; transcendence
grace 22, 32, 48
  as gift 78, 86, 88, 96
  and sacraments 33–5
Graham, Elaine, Walton, Heather and Ward, Frances 130, 131–2, 133 n.18
Gregory the Great, pastoral theology 143–4, 145, 146
Gregory of Nazianzus 24, 36 n.6, 66, 71
Gregory of Nyssa 36 n.6
Gregory Palamas 142
Grenz, Stanley 43–4
Guenther, Margaret 5, 171–3

guidance 6
guilt, and salvation 79–80, 82, 111
Guite, Malcolm 32

heart, and prayer 51
heresies, and nature of Christ 63–4, 68–9
Hildegard of Bingen 137–8, 155
Hill, Christopher 149–50
Hoare, Liz 93, 120, 122
holding:
  by God 27
  in direction 58–9, 75
holiness 93, 111, 113
Holmes, Stephen 120
Holy Communion, as encounter with God 34
Holy Spirit:
  and baptism in the Spirit 99–100, 108–9
  and companionship 99–118
  and creativity 103–6, 125
  as experience 99–100, 109
  gifts of 106–8, 109–110
  and immanence of God 111–12
  and inspiration 103–6, 125–8
  and mission 21, 99, 116–17
  as personal 100–102, 108
  and spiritual direction 99–118, 126–7, 135, 139
Hooker, Richard 31

INDEX OF NAMES AND SUBJECTS

Hopkins, Gerard Manley 29
hospitality:
　of God 19, 23, 103
　of scripture 124–5
　spiritual direction as 5, 26, 34
Hughes, Gerard 146
human beings:
　as beings-in-communion 43–5, 46, 50–1, 52, 56, 59
　holistic approach to 50–51
　psychological approaches to 54–9, 60, 131
humility 107, 138, 141, 171, 179
Hunt, William Holman 87

identification, and incarnation 66–8
Ignatius of Loyola, *Spiritual Exercises* 8, 115, 132, 144–6, 150
illumination, and redemption 51, 91–3, 96, 143, 180, 183
image of God 16, 30, 43–5, 46–7, 52, 60, 103
　restored in baptism 71, 72
imagination, and use of scripture 131–2, 133 n.18
immanence of God 101, 111–12
incarnation:
　and body 17, 62–4, 66–7, 68–70, 82
　and empathy 64–6

and identification 66–8
and rescue 81
and salvation 88
individualism 11, 43, 79, 96, 115–16
inspiration:
　and Holy Spirit 103–6, 125–8
　of scripture 125–8
　and spiritual direction 104–6
Irenaeus of Lyons 20–21

Jeff, Gordon 166–8
Jesuits:
　approaches to spiritual direction 8–9
　and scripture 128
Jesus:
　as being-in-communion 68
　as God incarnate 61–76
　as human and divine 62–4, 66–7, 68–9, 70–2, 76, 126
John of the Cross 92
John of Damascus 24
judgement, and sin 79–80, 97, 111
Julian of Norwich 80
Jung, Carl 55, 56–7, 59

Keller, Tim 24–5
Kelsey, David 45
Kendrick, Graham 23
kenosis (self-emptying), in direction 65, 67, 73–4

Kirk, Kenneth 20–21
Klein, Melanie 58
knowledge:
 as *poiesis* 10, 12–13, 18, 139
 as *praxis* 10, 12–13, 18, 139, 175, 181
 as *theoria* 10, 11, 139
knowledge of God 9, 11–13, 19–22, 26
 and illumination 92–3
 through sacraments 33–5, 40, 96
 through scripture 30–33, 40

Lane, Belden 131
language:
 and gender 36–7, 102–3, 117–18
 limitations 81
 and textuality 151
Lectio Divina 31–2, 127
Leech, Kenneth 3, 4, 6, 8, 11, 14, 15, 139, 148, 187
letter-writing 137–8, 139, 143
liberation 13–15, 50–2, 116–17, 132, 134
liberation theology 67
light, divine 91–3
Lings, George 14
Lollard movement 152, 153

Malphurs, Aubrey 184
Maule, Graham and Bell, John 23
Merton, Thomas 38 n.7, 50, 57, 163
Milton, John 79
mindfulness 95
mission:
 and the Church 14–15, 33, 159–60, 162, 185–6
 Five Marks 70 n.9, 79
 and Holy Spirit 21, 99, 116–17
Moltmann, Jürgen 24, 88
monastic tradition 123–4, 148–9, 155
 and Reformation 148–9
 and Rules 140–1, 146–7
mutuality, spiritual 152–4
Myers-Briggs Type Indicator (MBTI) 55–6
mystical tradition 26, 92, 93–5

Narrative Theology, Canonical 133 n.18
Nouwen, Henri 27

object relations theory 58
O'Brien, Kevin SJ 145
Oliver, Gordon 120, 123–5, 126–8, 130, 131
Otto, Rudolf 101

Panciera, Silvana 147–8
participation 115–16
Pelikan, Yaroslav 137
penance and reconciliation 90

INDEX OF NAMES AND SUBJECTS

perichoresis 24, 26
personality types 54–5, 184–5
Peterson, Eugene 24
philokalia 139
phronesis, as practical wisdom 10, 13, 18, 163
place, liminal 12, 73–5, 83
poiesis 10, 12–13, 18, 139
praxis 10, 12–13, 18, 139, 175, 181
prayer:
  contemplative 48–9, 53, 95, 129, 163
  as conversation 37–40
  psychology of 54–8, 59, 60
  public 163
  silent 48–9, 52, 110
  and spiritual direction 3–4, 7, 170–71
presence of God 19–20, 23, 38, 82–5, 95, 109
  and attunement 113–14, 117
  and beauty 30
  and direction 49, 52, 62–3, 117, 127–8
  as gift 85–6
  and recognition 114–15
  and sacraments 33–5, 96
  and threshold 73, 78, 83–4, 89, 91, 97
  and the Trinity 24–5, 44
  and the Word 30–33
pride 79
professionals, directors as 171–3, 176
psychology:
  interpersonal psychodynamics 58–9, 131
  of prayer 54–8, 59, 60
  purgation, and redemption 89–90, 96, 97, 143, 180, 183

ransom, and atonement 87–8
recognition 114–15
reconciliation:
  and the cross 81–2
  and penance 90
redemption 87
  and illumination 91–3, 96, 143, 180, 183
  and purgation 89–90, 96, 97, 143, 180, 183
  and union with God 91, 93–7, 143, 180, 183
Reed, Angela, Osmer, Richard and Smucker, Marcus 9, 168
Reformation, and monastic tradition 148–9
Reiser, William SJ 9
relationship:
  in direction 5–7, 15, 42, 45, 49, 52, 58–9
  with God 3, 19–22, 25, 37, 39, 44, 47, 50–51
  within the Trinity 22–3, 24–5, 44
rescue, salvation as 61–3, 70, 77–8, 80, 81, 86, 97
revelation of God 33–5, 182

Richard of Chichester 97
Roderick, Philip 38 n.7
Rohr, Richard 57, 163 n.29
Rolle, Richard 91–2
Rublev, Andrei, *Icon of the Holy Trinity* 25–6
rule of life 70, 140–41, 146–8, 170

sacraments:
  Church as 151
  and knowledge of God 33–5, 96
  and scripture 128–30
sacrifice, and sin 87–8
St Patrick's breastplate 62
salvation:
  and creation 70
  and the cross 81–2
  as experiential 77–8
  as gift 78, 82–6
  God as 45, 47, 86–8
  and guilt 79–80, 82, 111
  as process 78
  as rescue 61–3, 70, 77–8, 80, 81, 86, 97
  and scripture 123
  and transformation 77–98, 111–12, 132
sanctification, entire 108
Sattler, Michael 152
Schillebeeckx, Edward 33–4
Schroeder, Roger 24
scripture:
  and atonement 87
  authority of 122–5, 136, 150
  as drama 127–8, 133–6
  and experience 130–2
  historical criticism 127
  inspiration 125–8
  and knowledge of God 30–3
  as narrative 132–4
  as sacrament 128–30
  and sin 79–80
  in spiritual direction 119–36, 150–51
  theological approaches to 119–36
self, true 50–1, 55, 57
Senge, Peter et al. 85
sexuality 52–3, 68–9
Sheldrake, Philip 59
silence:
  in prayer 48–9, 52, 89, 110
  in spiritual direction 49, 108
Simeon Stylites 142
sin 83
  and confession 89–91
  as disordered desire 46–9, 50, 60
  of individuals and communities 78–9
  and judgement 79–80, 97, 111
  and sacrifice 87–8
soul friendship 6, 148
speaking in tongues 100, 109–10, 116
Spencer, Stanley 70
spiritual direction:

INDEX OF NAMES AND SUBJECTS

and approaches to scripture 119–36, 150–1
boundaries 59, 67–8, 75, 121, 167
and the Church 157–76
and confession 166
contemporary context 14–16, 164–6
corporate 183–5
as craft 10–11, 13, 16, 18, 173, 174, 176
definitions 1–4
for every Christian? 166–71
and gifts 106–8
growth and development 138–9
hiddenness 64–5, 175
and Holy Spirit 99–118, 126–7, 135, 139
inter-disciplinary approaches 53–4, 131
Jesuit approaches 8–9
and liminal space 73–5, 83
metaphors for 4–5, 7, 18, 62–3, 173, 177
in monastic tradition 140–1, 148–9
and nomenclature 5–7
oversight of 164–6
and practical theology 1, 2, 4, 9–13, 119–20, 158, 177–87
and prayer 3–4, 7
sources 7–9
turning up for 65, 76

spirituality, Ignatian 8, 132, 144–6
substitution, and atonement 86
suffering and evil 39, 40–1, 79, 82–3
supervision, for directors 53, 58, 67–8, 120, 143, 164–5, 175, 176

Taylor, John V. 21
techne (skill) 11, 13
Teresa of Ávila 92, 95
textuality 149–51
theology:
  espoused 119, 120, 122, 136
  natural 28, 29
  operant 119, 120–1, 122–3, 130, 135–6
  pastoral 143–4
  systematic 12, 21, 181, 183
theology, practical:
  and confession 90
  and prayer 4
  and spiritual direction 1, 2, 4, 9–13, 119–20, 158, 177–87
Theophan the Recluse 142
theoria 10, 11, 139
theosis 17, 26, 71, 76, 94
Thomas, Gabby 71 n.10
Thomas, R. S. 105
Thompson, Francis 84
Thornton, Martin 4–5, 8, 11, 14, 15, 69

threshold, and presence of God 73, 78, 83–4, 89, 91, 97
Tilby, Angela 48–9
Tillich, Paul 130
time, liminal 74–5
tongues, speaking in 100, 109–10, 116
Torr, Stephen 39
Tracy, David 130
traditions of the Church 123–4, 137–56
  monastic tradition 123–4, 140–1, 148
transcendence of God 35, 101
transformation:
  and Paschal mystery 72, 75–6
  and salvation 77–98, 111–12, 132
Trinity 22–6, 62
  encounters with 27–8
  as immanent and economic 36
  interrelationship 22–3, 24–5, 44, 147
  see also Christ; God; Holy Spirit
Tyndale, William 81

Ulanov, Ann and Ulanov, Barry 59
unconscious, the 49, 56–7
union with God 91, 93–7, 143, 180, 183

van Ruusbroec, Jan 94–5
via negativa see apophatic tradition
vita apostolica 147–8
Volmar (friend of Hildegard of Bingen) 138, 155

Walls, Andrew 160 n.24
Ware, Kallistos 143
Warren, Rick 183
Wells, Sam 32, 65, 133–5
Wesley, John 85–6, 153
Whitehead, James and Whitehead, Evelyn Eaton 193
Williams, Rowan 158
Wink, Walter 183
Winnicott, Donald 59
wisdom, practical 10, 12, 163, 175
wonder 30
Word of God 30–33, 102
Wright, N.T. (Tom) 32, 133
Wright, Stephen 18
writing, popular devotional texts 149–51
Wycliffe, John 152

Yeats, W. B. 83
Yoder, John H. 152
Young, Frances 35
Young, William 102

Zizioulas, John 23, 43–4

www.ingramcontent.com/pod-product-compliance
Lightning Source LLC
Chambersburg PA
CBHW020905080526
44589CB00011B/449